COMING HOME

COMING HOME

Reclaiming America's Conservative Soul

Ted V. McAllister & Bruce P. Frohnen

BOOKS

New York · London

First American edition published in 2019 by Encounter Books,
an activity of Encounter for Culture and Education, Inc.,
a nonprofit, tax exempt corporation.
Encounter Books website address: www.encounterbooks.com

Manufactured in the United States and printed on
acid-free paper. The paper used in this publication meets
the minimum requirements of ANSI / NISO Z39.48—1992
(R 1997) (*Permanence of Paper*).

FIRST AMERICAN EDITION

LIBRARY OF CONGRESS CATALOGING-IN-PUBLICATION DATA

Names: McAllister, Ted V., author. | Frohnen, Bruce, author.
Title: Coming home : reclaiming America's conservative soul /
by Ted V. McAllister and Bruce P. Frohnen.
Description: New York : Encounter Books, [2019] | Includes bibliographical
references and index.
Identifiers: LCCN 2018055428 (print) | LCCN 2019002283 (ebook) |
ISBN 9781641770576 (ebook) | ISBN 9781641770569 (hardcover : alk.
paper)
Subjects: LCSH: Conservatism—United States. | United States—Politics and
government--Philosophy. | United States—Social policy—Philosophy.
Classification: LCC JC573.2.U6 (ebook) | LCC JC573.2.U6 M358 2019
(print) |
DDC 320.520973—dc23
LC record available at https://lccn.loc.gov/2018055428

CONTENTS

PART II: REBUILDING OUR CULTURAL HOME
The Return to Human Nature

FOR OUR LITTLE PLATOONS.

For Dena, Elisabeth, and Lukas – T. V. M.

*For Gloria Antonia, Michaela Isobel,
and Augustine Burke* – B. P. F.

Introduction

The peaceful era of global prosperity declared at the end of the Cold War has ended, if indeed it ever began. We have entered a time of deep cultural conflict forced to the political surface by unprecedented economic dislocation and social change. From serious questions about the viability of the European Union to fits of highly dangerous nationalism in Russia and China, geopolitics bespeaks nothing so clearly as system collapse. Peoples and governments are in crisis.

Even in the United States these forces are at work. The levels of panic evident among so many Americans at the election of Donald Trump, which have continued well into his presidency, are a clear sign of a crisis in our political, social, and even cultural life. Americans' lack of trust in our political system, in each other, and in the decency of our way of life are undermining our ability to function as a people. And this distrust stems from deeper, more frightening causes; it is a painful eruption from a civilizational disease. A civilization is diseased when its people lose faith in its essential ideals and institutions, and when its elite loses or distorts its historical memory. This disease eventually produces an ersatz culture so alien to genuine human needs that the people come to lose the feeling of home – of belonging and attachment – that is any culture's lived reality. Years of leftist attacks on time-honored institutions that have served to knit a nation of patriots and friends out of America's rich pluralism, combined with a progressive case of historical dementia, have robbed many Americans of our cultural home, our distinctive, rooted, and beautiful tradition as a self-ruling and self-respecting people.

Our ancestors have been turned into a rogues' gallery of exploiters and their countless victims – a past that our cultural elite tells us is so shameful that loyalty to any of its cultural bequests makes us automatically complicit in the crimes that now constitute our only patrimony. In a civilizational sense, our elite has left us without cultural forebears; they have made us orphans.

Orphans can still find home, security, and the conditions for happiness so long as they retain institutions serving their most human needs. All humans need stable families to help us develop a strong sense of belonging and attachment. We need local, face-to-face associations and institutions that help us form solid characters and secure our identities as persons and members of communities. And we need a sense of purpose linked with our identity. But we American orphans confront an elite culture that, in the name of liberating the individual, dissolves the institutions and structures that help form stable identities. Instead of a cultural home capacious enough to shelter natives and orphans, we have been left with a perverse species of individualism, stripping from us the relationships that give us strength and meaning. The childish rebellion for so long sold to us as "liberation" has alienated us from our spouses, neighbors, and communities, leaving us "free" from that which makes life worth living.

The crisis of our time, then, might be called homelessness. Homelessness, in the way we mean it here, is a separation from our true nature or our true selves. To rebuild America requires that we reclaim our heritage and rethink our culture and institutions to allow the natural growth and revitalization of the cultural places where we find our natural home.

In writing this short work about reclaiming conservatism and its principles, we have made the assumption that you, in choosing to read it, already have some understanding of the contemporary crisis. Still, a quick overview of conditions on the ground may highlight key characteristics of the current malaise.

People can only be genuinely happy if they govern themselves, making choices based on an understanding of their full human needs. Those who "choose" to abuse drugs, or to use their fellow human beings as mere tools of their lust, greed, or feelings of superiority, cannot be truly happy because they are governed by their passions and lack decent character. Trapped in the pursuit of thrills, they lack the self-control and sense of proportion necessary to achieve any sense of satisfaction and genuine hope for the future.

Decent character requires social and cultural supports that help us to become good neighbors and citizens, and in turn to raise our children to be such. Most fundamentally, it requires strong families embedded in thick layers of associations and institutions. To rebuild our lives together we must protect and enliven the spirit of our civil society. But we have material needs as well. Most crucially, people need dignified, productive work so that they can support their families to be part of self-reliant communities and associations. Without both dignified work and meaningful civic engagement, communities crumble, turning self-reliance and happiness into lingering illusions from a desiccated past.

For decades, now, political elites have promised to help our families. Yet, even as our governments take on greater power, they become ever more remote from those they claim to represent and serve. A colossal regulatory system commands our civil society, homogenizing rules, social norms, and the people themselves; it increasingly takes over the roles, the autonomy, and even the purpose of the associations in which we once learned the art, necessity, and rewards of self-rule. This tutelary government (the classic "nanny state") actively cooperates with globalized crony capitalism to enforce a perverse individualism rooted in meaningless consumption and fluid identities, robbing us of the means of becoming a happy, self-governing people.

Individualism alienates us from community, from a serious connection with tradition, and from our true selves. The "liberation" of individualism steals from us our birthright to belong to, and participate in, a rich community of memory and purpose and to derive from our social order the resources to become distinctive, mature persons. Without thick communities that attach people to others by way of shared memories, obligations, freedoms, and the special affection or love that comes from belonging to one another, "liberated" individuals – which is to say alienated people – stand politically naked before the government. Eventually we are left with the soft despotism about which Alexis de Tocqueville warned us, in which the state becomes our "schoolmaster" and exercises "an immense tutelary power" – a power that is "absolute, detailed, regular"* and far-seeing, even if deceptively mild. Individualism leads not to freedom, but to the absence of maturity or character; it leads us to retreat into an intensely private world, a tiny space in which we may exercise our singular, feckless will.

---

* Alexis de Tocqueville, *Democracy in America*, trans. and ed. Harvey C. Mansfield and Delba Winthrop (Chicago: University of Chicago Press, 2000), 663.

Of course, those with power have more room for the effective exercise of their wills. Today's new economic class, disconnected from local or even national allegiances, creates and profits from globalizing regulations and policies. This globalization circumvents elected legislative control and undermines workers' self-mastery, even as it corrodes the very idea of loyalty and mutual obligation. Members of our ruling class, smug in the self-serving belief that their power and wealth are merited by their technological and economic productivity, have come to think of themselves as the anointed agents of transformation. Abetted by huge and interlocking institutions of propaganda, the provincial elites of this class, removed from any historical imagination or recognition of the rich inheritance that has empowered their accomplishments, fetishize a utopian world as surely as would any devout Communist.

The disorientation of our times, and the anger attending it, is the result of rapid structural changes stemming from this new globalism. Those outside the ruling elite experience an incomprehensible world of rapid and unpredictable change. From workplaces that once fostered self-reliance, to communities increasingly hollowed out by despair and redundancy, to venerated beliefs made into objects of ridicule by constant "progressive" preaching in the classroom, the press, and government, all that used to be safe and understandable has been rendered toxic and bewildering.

Little wonder that people "want their country back" even if they have no clear idea what that means. They experience loss and a palpable sense that their society is becoming alien, no longer legible or predictable or supportive. Feeling powerless, people also are unscripted. Before this new globalist age, most of us recognized that we belonged to a national story that incorporated shared values, beliefs, and purposes. Belonging to a shared story, we were connected by webs of association including family, neighbors, coffee shop friends, fellow workers, and even employers. A palpable sense of collective identity allowed America's "little platoons" to be tangible, idiosyncratic, and diverse, while also knitting them into a narrative of shared historical memory. Without the bonds of memory there is no nation.

As we see it, this is our crisis in a nutshell. We believe that American conservatism offers the best hope to reclaim American civilization and our rightful gifts as heirs to that civilization. However, we write at a time when "conservatism" is a confused and disordered category and when the leaders of the "conservative movement" themselves are confounded by and complicit in the cultural deracination and ideological madness we've described.

To move forward we must begin by reclaiming America's conservative soul. American conservatism represents the most deeply American set of principles. But these have been lost or distorted in recent years, and so require a fresh history to remind us of who we are as inheritors of American civilization.

Our argument develops in two related parts – a reclaiming of our history and a reminder of our human nature. Part I of this book is a narrative history of conservatism in America. Only in Part II do we address contemporary issues as manifestations of our historical forgetting, seeking to remind ourselves and our readers of our true historical nature. We proceed in this manner because historical consciousness – grasping the reality that we exist within traditions that shape what we see and what we become – is central to human nature. And awareness of this nature is central to traditional conservatism.

Our History and Our Nature

In Part I, our historical account sustains seven key claims:

(1) American conservatism is a living tradition that emerged out of English traditions of common law and inherited liberties, the deep influence of Dissenting Protestantism and the covenanting tradition, and an almost instinctive empiricism that trusts experience over abstract rationality. These are our common roots.

(2) Even before nationhood, Americans' approaches to their circumstances, conflicts, and ways of life had developed into two overlapping intellectual traditions – liberalism and conservatism.

(3) The United States Constitution expresses fittingly, and better than any other document, the compromises between and common ground of these two American traditions.

(4) Conservatism is the most powerfully American tradition because conservatives seek to preserve American principles and norms, and to improve them as conditions warrant.

(5) In part as a reaction to powerful global trends, an American ideology hostile to all American intellectual traditions – progressivism – emerged in the twentieth century with the aim of transforming the nation according to a conceptual blueprint going by the name of social justice.

(6) Rapid and unparalleled changes in geopolitics surrounding the Cold War created conditions that pushed conservatives to

reformulate their tradition as a more ahistorical, narrowly political, and even ideological version of itself.

(7) A new phase of economic globalization and the development of a politically potent form of American progressivism have made the ahistorical, ideological, and simplified form of conservatism both ineffective and ill-suited to the deepest American traditions reemerging in our time.

These claims serve as context for understanding our call for a form of American conservatism that is rooted in human nature, human purposes, and reinvigoration of the traditions within which communities may form and individual persons may lead good lives. By explaining the history of American conservatism, we urge our fellow Americans to reclaim their deepest traditions, much battered by political centralization and cultural atomization, but very much alive in the fabric of the American people. *We do not invent, we lay claim to our rightful inheritance.*

But we have a yet deeper reason for telling this history. American conservatism doesn't just "have" a history. Thinking historically is a defining characteristic of conservatives. Conservatives recognize that we are not born fully formed – equipped by nature for life – and that we inherit more than we can possibly recognize. We inherit language, art, science, and technology. We inherit liberties and laws, order and culture. And we inherit sins and lingering failures from our ancestors. We all are born situated and then are shaped by a process of acculturation. Unlike other animals, who cannot pass down such accomplishments, we humans, of any given generation or any given culture, are who we are in great measure because of what we inherited from folk we will never know. Only humans are historical animals – only humans can or need to think historically to be fully ourselves.

Traditional conservatism is very far from the claim that our actions are somehow determined by some vague entity known as history, let alone the claim that truth itself is relative. Historical consciousness is, in fact, a secure means of coming to grasp and preserve our understanding of the "permanent things," to borrow from T. S. Eliot. Humans live in awareness of a natural order that we neither define nor control and to which we seek to attune ourselves. The contrast with ideologues, who seek human empowerment untethered to purpose or design, is profound. All ideologies are characterized by abstract and universal claims that are suited to a narrow rationalism but ill-suited to human experience. Conservatives use reason and experience to understand the created universe of which we are a part, the moral commands placed on our own nature, and the sorts of arrangements that are suited to our nature.

Part I tells a history. Beyond that story's particulars, it seeks to show the essential role played by experience and tradition in allowing humans, within their limited cultural horizons, to perceive and understand universal moral principles. Because humans live in a constantly changing environment, conservatives must find ways to remain faithful to developed principle under altered conditions. Thus Part I is also the story of how conservatives have identified, refined, and articulated conservative principles – principles of natural law, ultimately – as they have emerged from concrete experience. Nothing in the first part of our book suggests that the principles change, and, in fact, in Part II we present arguments from nature, from ends or goals, and from predetermined purpose. American conservatives understand experience and historical consciousness as means through which humans may apprehend, hold close, and put into action the moral principles of a good society.

We all belong to a normative order that we did not create.

We also participate in living communities, made up of specific relationships and norms that constitute the most cherished and enduring parts of our identities. We belong to the natural order of things through the specific stories we each inhabit. The great danger of our time – the danger to keep in mind as you read the chapters that follow – is that we will lose our stories, that "each man [will] forget his ancestors . . . [and hide] his descendants from him," to quote Tocqueville.** This history-lessness is the necessary condition for the sort of tyranny that we moderns face – in which race, class, or some other abstract general characteristic is used as an excuse to destroy the relationships that make life worth living. We must understand not only the context of our time, but also our historical nature and its relationship to our most cherished ideals. Our tradition as a self-governing people cannot survive the rationalistic, ahistorical categories being foisted on us in the name of a false democracy and a false social justice. Our self-rule must be rooted in our story and embraced as our inheritance.

Rebuilding Our Cultural Home:
The Return to Human Nature

Like all people, Americans live in associations. Based on common goals, these associations take shape as responses to human needs within the circumstances of life in specific times and places. We help each other out with the needs of raising children; we worship together; we form civic groups to improve our towns; we band together as workers in a given field. What binds

---

** Tocqueville, *Democracy in America*, 484.

such associations together, and makes them work, is what Alexis de Tocqueville called mores. Mores are social habits, assumptions, and shared values that make up a kind of cultural instinct, a way of approaching community life that took a specific shape in America. Our physical, social, and historical circumstances forged American mores in a way that made our communities strong, resilient, and adaptive. They encouraged development of self-ruling characters and self-governing communities. This is our inheritance: it makes us who we are.

The American tradition encourages us to retain our inheritance while adapting it to new circumstances. This goes not just for communities and institutions but also for the mores that bind them. Mores change very slowly in a society that takes its guidance from experience, but institutions and relationships must change constantly, even if only in small, specific ways. When a significant set of institutions and associations no longer serves members' needs, conservatives are forced back to first principles; they must ask serious questions about human needs and human nature. At moments of institutional crisis, conservatives refine and articulate principles gleaned from their traditions, using them to adapt inherited institutions to changed conditions. Part I relates several moments in our history when such principles (rather than abstract dogmas) were gleaned and refined so as to maintain the continuity of our way of life. Because we are today in another crisis, Part II offers just such a stock-taking of our needs and our nature in the context of the American story.

If power is no longer in the hands of the people, if the people no longer govern themselves in their communities, then our way of life, our deepest values and the institutions in which they are lived, are vulnerable to outside powers. Today, we approach these conditions. The most dangerous and effective outside power in America goes by the name of progressivism. The elite purveyors of this ideology employ abstract claims to universal ("social") justice, demanding that the national government transform our nation of peoples, of semi-independent communities, associations, and institutions, into a homogeneous, equal society that "liberates" individuals from the sources of their own most natural identities. In place of a formed identity connected to their deepest human needs, the resulting alienated individuals craft shifting selves out of their desires and unformed wills. Such individuals are now beyond the reach of the authority of family, church, community, and other natural groups, instead finding themselves at the mercy of a distant, paternal government.

Individualism in America has been fostered and even demanded by powerful ideological forces occupying both political parties and the commanding heights of our culture. As a result, the federal government has taken an ever greater role in our lives, undermining and crowding out the associations that make up the body of American conservatism. And, because the network of associations and institutions in which good characters are formed and find expression has been torn asunder, our mores have been made vulnerable to direct assault by the ideological dogmas of progressivism. Millions of people who used to be at home in well-grounded institutions and communities are now disconnected and alienated. Their alienation has driven them to find solace in fleeting pleasures, and it has left these people unnaturally attracted to the infantilizing distractions of desire, pleasure, and security offered by politicians and their national government programs. Having lost the experience of self-rule and self-reliance, today's alienated citizens find it easy to surrender their hollowed-out communities in exchange for the life of "liberated" dependence promised by the tutelary state.

America must reclaim its conservative soul. To do this we must fight to rebuild our communities and associations, and to reclaim the collective freedom of communities to craft new institutions suited to their real needs and fitted to their local conditions. Part II examines specific American institutions, points out how progressive policies and attitudes have undermined them, and suggests how we might reclaim them by enlivening conservative mores and an understanding of what is demanded by our natures and natural goals.

American society's historical equilibrium of *e pluribus unum*, of unity within diversity, suffers most from a drive to centralize power and responsibility in a distant, national government claiming to provide for our needs and wants. In the name of economic security and "fairness," progressives have constructed a vast national apparatus of power and responsibility. Using this apparatus, the central government commands the people to act in specific ("just") ways and deprives them of the responsibility to order their own lives together. As a result, our local communities have been denied their very reason to exist. From the essential means by which we govern ourselves, localities have become mere corrupt appendages of a centralized machine controlling the most important aspects of our lives. To reclaim our way of life requires that we reclaim our right to govern ourselves, first and foremost by denying to the central government its power and authority to govern us "for our own good."

Part II makes six overall claims about what Americans must understand and do to reclaim their civilizational home:

(1) We must reclaim township government as the foundation of self-government in America. The freedom of communities to govern themselves must again be recognized as prior to and

more important than the rights of alienated individuals to follow their passions wherever they may lead.

(2) Within townships, the family is the single most important natural association. It is the community in which character is formed, in which we become who we will be, for better or worse. Attempts to "redefine" the family really are ways by which political elites use the government to take over its natural, primary role. We must insist that the natural family's structure and its proper goals of supporting and rearing children of good character be recognized as the foundation of any good society.

(3) Humans by nature are religious animals who yearn for higher meaning and who form communities to pursue this meaning through common worship and common modes of life. Denied or trained out of their natural belief in a higher power, people will transfer their faith either to the state or to their own fantasies and desires. We must reverse progressives' attempts to purge our specific American religious principles and traditions from our public discourse, from our communities, and from our law so that we may regain the social trust on which societies rely, the essentials of the common law on which our tradition rests, and the higher meaning that alone can allow us to order our own lives.

(4) One of a national government's truly essential tasks is that of defending that nation's borders. All peoples have a natural right and duty to sustain themselves and flourish by insisting that those who would join with them obey existing rules for membership and demonstrate a determination to adopt the fundamental norms of that nation. Citizenship in America comes – or ought to come if we are to remain Americans – with

expectations that one becomes attached to associations and local communities and brings the richness of one's own cultural inheritance into the host culture. Our always present and ever-evolving cultural diversity allows new citizens to contribute through the institutions and values of self-rule and self-reliance, beginning with the family and extending to, for example, Little Leagues, unions, and PTAs and eventually to an affection for a national story in which new citizens contribute their own particularities to the emerging chapter. Most of all, a nation's approach to immigration and new citizens must focus not on preventing change but on what we might call cultural sustainability. In America this cultural sustainability is not found in strict adherence to some creed but in dedication to the network of associations that maintains continuity with our past as it adapts to changing circumstances.

(5) Seeking their own power and pursuing an ideological vision of utopia, international elites are producing a globalist technocracy that destroys the economic independence of families and local communities. Protected and subsidized by government policies that favor economic power on an inhuman scale, globalist conglomerates must be brought back down to an appropriate size, with an appropriate level of power, so that people acting in their own communities may regain control over their economic lives.

(6) No self-governing people can afford to hand over its children to be educated by hostile elites. Several generations having been brought up under a national system of education that uses accrediting agencies and massive tax-supported endowments to put itself above local control and market forces, Americans find themselves in the difficult position of hoping that their

children will "grow out" of their education before it destroys their own lives or their society as a whole. Reclaiming our society, and our conservative soul, requires that we reclaim local control over our children's education and break the monopoly on educational power currently held by mutually supporting networks of bureaucrats, administrators, and leftist educators.

In Part II we call for concrete reforms aimed at reestablishing America's traditional structure as a community of self-governing communities. Some of these reforms may seem radical because they rest on a return to human nature currently suppressed and opposed by ideological elites. But our nature, despite being obscured by decades of hostility and corruption, does not and cannot disappear. We can, in fact, reclaim our rightful home in a society of interlocking, self-governing communities if we recognize and act on our true nature. Once we do so, we can reconnect with the tradition that grew out of our interaction with America's unique circumstances.

PART I

OUR HISTORY AND OUR NATURE

CHAPTER ONE

Who We Are
The American Tradition

America is a land – a geographical place of beauty and wonder. America is also a nation – a political system whose norms apply in this land. Most fundamentally, America is a people – a stunning variety of persons, families, and communities interacting at churches, in the marketplace, and in all the local associations of civic life. Americans differ from one another in many ways but join in valuing the dignity associated with a self-governing people and the pursuit of happiness in the context of a well-ordered social and communal life.

American conservatism by definition is dedicated to preserving and enriching America and the traditions that sustain it. Conservatism has never been the only voice in America, but it is the most distinctively American voice, emerging from the practices, customs, norms, and dispositions of a people that has formed and developed through the interaction of a specific history with equally specific circumstances. Our task in this era of ideology – of simplistic slogans and attempts to "fundamentally transform" our way of life – is to reclaim our culture. Reclamation begins with social and cultural retention: preserving for our descendants our most important civilizational accomplishments. Retention requires a deep affection for who we are together and what we have inherited. But the essential capacity

to retain, and to pass down what has been retained, is hardest
to cultivate and practice during times of rapid and disorienting
change, such as we are in now. To reclaim our most important
principles, therefore, we must innovate, bringing the principles
earned from past experiences into line with new conditions.

American conservatism is rooted in English tradition; its earliest principles emerged from the consolidation of accomplishments within English political and legal cultures. The defining
principles of this tradition are the product of empirical and historical knowledge; its temperament moderate, skeptical, hopeful but worldly; its method scientific and cognizant of the limits
of our knowledge; its passion ordered liberty. The conservative
tradition is never completely new because it concentrates on
retaining the best of what it has inherited. As a philosophical
tradition, then, American conservatism is best characterized as
the process of identifying, articulating, and refining principles
both gleaned by natural reason and revealed by Jewish and
Christian scriptures, but perfected and specified as norms
growing out of English, and then American, experiences.

American conservatism is thus uniquely American, though
its fountainhead is English. Its defining principles are the result
of retaining and refining America's English inheritance for
Americans, suited to American realities, and fitted to the pluralism of the American people. To understand American conservatism we must first rediscover these historical threads. How
did Americans shape their inheritance into the most successful
self-governing culture in human history?

More than perhaps any other people, the English from very
early times saw law as an expression and enforcement of preexisting customs. Both courts and juries saw justice, in court
at least, as vindication of the reasonable expectations of the
parties; the victor should be the person who has acted in a man-

ner most closely conforming to expected norms. Recognizing people's right to not be surprised by new rules, decrees, or ways of doing things, the law demanded that changes in customs be as gradual and naturally occurring as possible. The idea of "judge-made law" was foreign to the common law because the court's job was to find and enforce already existing understandings of proper conduct and of essential terms like "negligence," "property," and "due process" rather than to create them. This meant that law itself came to be seen as an expression of the people's will, expressed in action over time.

By the sixteenth century, the common law had developed into a product of reflection and refinement, most famously through the work of Edward Coke. It reflected the norms of the people as they emerged from actual practice, rooted in, rather than mechanically derived from, understandings of higher law, customs, and the requirements of the public good. Over time the common law would develop a theory of "precedent," whereby the decisions of previous courts would guide those of later ones. Previous examples would both limit and empower judges as they addressed the emerging needs of new circumstances, the general requirements of due process, and the particular needs of plural communities.

If the common law emerged through slow accretions of precedent and by way of reflection and intellectual refinement, the articulation of conservative principles in a more general way emerged most powerfully in revolutions, which served as historical moments of clarification. The word "revolution," derived from the Latin *revolvere*, meaning to turn or roll back, entered European discourse as an astronomic term concerning the natural course of planets orbiting the sun; when it was applied to political life in reference to England's Glorious Revolution of 1688, it conveyed the idea of reclaiming. Understood this way,

English tradition was marked by a series of restatements of traditional rights, along with institutional reforms intended to better preserve these rights. Whether in Magna Carta from 1215, the Petition of Right from 1628, or the Declaration of Right from 1689, English constitutional declarations forged a tradition played out in the American Declaration of Independence. The bulk of all these documents is taken up with a list of charges against an overreaching king whose innovations threatened inherited rights and liberties. The rebellious English barons, Parliament, and the American Continental Congress all refined and affirmed what was already theirs – they "rolled back" to preserve but also to solidify their inheritance. Changes in the powers of the king and even secession from the British Empire were seen as necessary for the conservation of ordered liberty.

Retention and innovation are necessarily linked for conservatives. Knowledge passed down is necessary to develop new knowledge, making innovation impossible without retention. But the opposite also is true. Because change is a human constant, though the speed of change varies dramatically, a society must be able to adjust, adapt, and find necessary innovations to preserve what is cherished, lest custom and tradition die. Indeed, when the normal course of life is threatened or collapses the effort at reclamation produces renewal; it yields discoveries of neglected or misunderstood parts of the living stream of experience that have become luminous in context and warrant the effort of articulating, refining, and defending them.

Anglo-American conservatism is deeply empirical and, when applied to politics, deeply historical because all real evidence on this subject is found in the historical record. The science of politics requires knowing a great deal about past policies, practices, and ideas and the experiences they generated. As shown in the constitutional debates between American Federalists and Anti-Federalists, history is a great storehouse, providing examples of what works and does not work under differing circumstances.

But conservatism's historical empiricism has a more important function. A deep knowledge of one's history provides a meaningful story about the world one occupies. This story is rich with examples and eccentricities and reveals that one lives in a social order suffused with peculiarities that make it unique in many ways and that show the contingency of every act and reaction. The complexity of this story makes one aware that things could have been different, that choices made based on the best knowledge of the time have unanticipated consequences, often taking many generations to play out. History helps one love the imperfect and odd society to which one belongs without demanding that it be something that it is not. Few principles are more important to American conservatism than the need to love the particular and the flawed over the abstract and apparently perfect.

This historical understanding provides a deep knowledge of one's nation and how it got to be what it is. Neither the jury trial nor property rights, for example, developed along any logical or rational line; they grew over the circuitous course of historical development, as have a myriad of beloved principles associated with one's own story, one's own land – even, or perhaps especially, if one has adopted this land as one's own and one is woven into the story. American rights, liberties, and practices come as a primarily cultural inheritance.

The story of America's hard-won and always precarious rights and liberties is complex, and its sheer complexity makes it all the more dear. The conservative cannot take lightly what is such a rare and beautiful flower. He comes to love his rights and liberties, as well as the morally complex story that gave them to him. The story he knows is the source of these cherished accomplishments, so he no more expects other peoples to have the same accomplishments than he expects other climates to produce the same crops. Finally, the history he knows so well provides ample evidence that the most beloved parts of his inheritance demand preservation, protection, and diligence.

Perhaps America's greatest inheritance is its constitutional tradition. The United States Constitution is imbued with the spirit of conservatism: reclamation and innovation. The Constitution and the Bill of Rights create specific protections for traditional English liberties as well as the innovative but experience-based American principle of freedom of religion. The framers understood the Constitution to be consistent with the common law – with the principles and rights articulated and developed within the system of customary law in England and America. The Constitution's structural novelties were designed to serve inherited principles of governance. Responding to rational fear that a unified government would abuse its power, the framers had to find a way to represent "the people" in all their complexity.

The Constitution arose, not from the desire to forge a "new nation," but from a determination to protect Americans' way of life by ceding limited and specified powers to a more robust "federal" government. The Constitution's complex governmental apparatus, with its separated powers and checks and balances intended to protect the people's rights and liberties, had only a limited charge, and only limited powers for carrying out that charge. The lion's share of governmental action would take place at the local level, within a system using the interests of states and the new national government to check one another. Within this new government, the legislative branch assumed the greatest powers and responsibilities, though limited to achieving specific ends concerned with national defense and the maintenance of peace and freedom of movement and commerce among the states. The legislative branch also provided internal checks between the immediate will of the majority as expressed in the House of Representatives and the interests of the states as expressed by their representatives in the Senate. The president was chosen indirectly by the Electoral College in a process meant to elicit the refined judgment of the people.

The US Constitution was not designed to express the general will of the people understood as a majority, nor was it crafted to make the federal government responsible for ruling for the common good as defined by politicians. Rather, it produced a government that mediates among various groups (states, economic interests, regional interests, and so on), promoting stability and prudent conduct by encouraging competing interests to check one another. Self-interest did not suggest the absence of a common good. Rather, the best interest of the nation is served by ensuring that governments provide a structure designed for a free people to pursue their lives in communities of purpose and interest without presuming the right to change other communities to fit their own ideas.

In all of these ways, the Constitution was an innovative system of government in support of inherited principles, rights, and liberties. It was, in short, conservative. The product of the most famous act of deliberation in the modern world, the document was wrought out of compromises that engaged principle and interest, that called on people to seek the good while recognizing limits, to be daring in preservation and prudent in innovation. No such creation could be without flaws – but then no frame of government issuing from dreams of solving all problems could possibly succeed in anything save tyranny. Prudence governed innovation, while a worldly understanding of self-interest produced innovations most conducive to the preservation of our most cherished liberties.

American conservatism is linked intimately to the Constitution because that Constitution is linked intimately to America – as a place, a government, a people. But not even the Constitution can sum up, let alone substitute for, the story that has made our way of life. The principles and inherited rights and liberties that developed from the origins of our common law have been under assault for many decades. The goal of these assaults is not merely a change in political structure; it is the elimination of America as a social, political, and cultural whole. To protect and reclaim our home requires first that we reclaim our understanding of how our rights and liberties are being lost and especially how conservatism has lost its connection to them.

CHAPTER TWO

American Conservatism

Conservatism in America emerged during the period around the Revolution and the Constitution's framing. This was a time of unusual intellectual flourishing in which important distinctions emerged out of a shared intellectual culture. These distinctions would eventually take shape as competing intellectual traditions, each rooted in the same Anglo-American intellectual culture and each committed, in different ways, to ordered liberty.

In late-eighteenth-century America, when the peoples of British North America were most conspicuous for their diversity, a shared intellectual culture facilitated philosophical, political, and moral conversation in which almost all participants drew from the same sources. Americans lived the motto they would later adopt – *e pluribus unum*, or "out of many, one." Although the colonists hailed from different sections of Britain and several European countries during an era when travel times and local habits made commerce and interaction unusual if not rare, came from different classes within the Old World's strict class hierarchies, and belonged to rival and sometimes hostile religious traditions, nonetheless they shared a common patrimony. The nine colonial colleges, for instance, displayed striking similarities in their curricula despite their denominational differences. All of them connected the provincial American student to the history, philosophy, and literature of Western civilization. Those who emerged from these institutions in the late eighteenth century knew a great deal about ancient history, particularly relating to political experiments, tyranny, and the fate of liberty. They were deeply immersed in Roman and other ancient thinkers. They were well versed in the intellectual flowering of the English and Scottish Enlightenment and thus knew well the great scientific leaps of recent centuries, including the developing idea that the universe displays physical "laws" only recently discovered by human inquiry. The members of the educated, ruling class all read and debated thinkers like John Locke, Montesquieu, and William Blackstone, and more contemporary thinkers like David Hume, Adam Smith, Thomas Reid, Adam Ferguson, and a host of Continental thinkers.

Americans also shared an identifiably Protestant view of the world. Whether orthodox Christians or Unitarians, American leaders saw individual choice as central to our moral agency. At the same time, they had internalized the idea and practice of covenanting relationships central to social life. People bound themselves before God in marriage, in business, in religious community, and in the founding of towns, states, and societies. Covenanting produced in Americans the ability to organize groups for purposes chosen freely and capable of requiring strong commitment from their members to the purposes of these groups. The requirements of life on the frontier undergirded and helped produce a specifically Protestant devotion to community, and to toleration and religious and intellectual freedom; with this Americans stressed the moral virtue of voluntary actions in doing good for one's neighbors. Ironically, devout and sectarian Protestants drew from their distinctive beliefs and experiences to produce towns that discerning observers like Alexis de Tocqueville would recognize as closely akin to medieval Catholic villages, with their strong communal identities and diversity of enlivening associations.

Finally, Americans worked within a version of Christian teachings recognizing each person's moral freedom and propensity toward destructive self-love. Great vigilance was required, then, to prevent abuse of power. More generally, a thick skein of institutions, habits, and communal supports was needed to induce people to live and act in their genuine self-interest and to check selfish tendencies. American intellectual leaders recognized that their inheritance of expansive individual and local liberties was fragile and dependent for its protection on religion, diverse institutions, thick communal obligations, and other social conditions, and that radical change threatened all of this.

Americans' common intellectual inheritance did not create uniformity of thought, but it enabled a deep and meaningful conversation and perhaps the greatest public act of deliberation in history, highlighted by, but not limited to, the debate over the US Constitution. Profound differences of opinion and theme emerged, but in a way that allowed understanding and engagement. Deep commonality allowed for useful difference, for a meaningful republic or commonwealth requires members who share enough to allow comprehension of, and even some admiration for, opinions they do not hold.

The richness of this shared intellectual culture, and the fluid ways its resources might be reimagined in new contexts, made the American founding especially fertile, helping it spawn both the conservative and liberal intellectual-political traditions. Conservatism and liberalism in America shared common roots in English commercial, legal, and religious practice. Conservatism emphasized the importance of historical ties and customary relations. Liberalism emphasized formal, often individual consent. Both recognized the necessity of social trust and ordered liberty. Neither was a narrow ideology in the contemporary partisan sense.

These traditions presented differing perspectives on a common patrimony. Consider, as a simple and obvious example, the influence of Locke. Locke's *Second Treatise of Government* makes an abstract, rationalist argument for the same rights that the English had long defended on empirical and historical grounds. The rights of life, liberty, and property are perfectly consistent with common law understandings and covenantal communities. However, Locke's method of apprehending and defending these rights, in sharp contrast to the common law, relies on a mythical "state of nature" inhabited by individuals who only institute political order through a self-conscious social contract. Largely ignored today but of central importance to emerging liberals in the late eighteenth century was Locke's insistence that the prepolitical order existed within a sacred horizon. Locke firmly asserted that the prepolitical or natural equality so important to his argument presumed God. God's authority enabled persons to employ their natural reason, producing artificial creations like government and law to protect their natural rights. And this natural reason itself was developed in family-based communities where, even in the state of nature, persons naturally associated and forged prepolitical associations.

The social contract idea is rich with competing meanings, and it is helpful to note that as these meanings change so also do the desired outcomes. If one stresses with Locke that the contract presumes a natural and prepolitical order of human relationships and culture, then the social contract supports the liberal tradition in America. But if the social contract begins with humans detached from any natural relationships or identifiers, then the essence of the contract that emerges is hostile to the authority or power of any natural, prepolitical institution or norms (culture). It was this form of social contract that would become the basis for a third American tradition hostile toward the first two, namely, progressivism. So, as we can see, Locke's influence on American thinkers was, and remains, complicated. Few Americans in the founding era would have thought themselves disciples of Locke, but almost all found parts of his argument authoritative, though for different reasons. To invoke Locke, as in the Declaration of Independence, was not to introduce contentious debate but rather to restate rhetorically powerful, inherited truisms regarding the importance of rights. This didn't make America or the founding Lockean; indeed, many other thinkers were more important in debates of the time, including the French thinker Montesquieu, the British lawyer Blackstone, and, of course, the Bible. But one group of thinkers, most closely associated with Thomas Paine and Thomas Jefferson, used Locke (among others) to develop an argument – owing nothing to convention – grounded in a rational, nonempirical assertion of moral truths.

Proponents of this liberal stream of thought sought the realization of human potential by liberating individuals from outside constraints, defining government as the protector of individual rights, and making toleration of differences the prime social value so that individuals would gain maximal freedom to define and construct their own lives. This liberal tradition stresses self-rule in terms drawn from Locke's social contract theory and recognizes in democracy the moral legitimacy of government by popular consent. And so, liberals emphasize the right of self-government (eventually focusing on majority rule or democracy) as tethered to the moral protections of individual rights that are universal and natural.

The resulting articulation of "liberal democracy" was meant

to balance majority power against the natural rights of individuals who often need government protection. Happiness, on this view, is a matter of individual empowerment. Each individual is to be liberated to pursue his happiness on his terms, within the constraints and definitions imposed by individualism and majority rule.

Another tradition, less attracted to Locke but not dismissive of him, also emerged from these resources. Conservatism would keep closer to English and Scottish empiricism – to Hume, Smith, and Edmund Burke – and to traditional understandings that emphasized the importance of religion and, in most cases, localism. Conservatives like John Adams, James Madison, and Alexander Hamilton pushed back against the abstract claims appropriated by Jefferson and others without rejecting other parts of Locke's philosophy. These conservatives were deeply suspicious of moral reasoning that avoids religious authority and doubted liberals' presumed trajectory of liberty leading to democracy. Instead, they stressed the fragility of the civilization they inhabited – and of all civilizations, for that matter. The networks of institutions and customs that had grown up in America and England fostered the sorts of self-restraining people who were well suited to self-rule and to the self-reliance and good character from which happiness derives. On this view, a healthy society that shapes self-ruling people prepares the way for happiness because its members possess the resources necessary to satisfy the deepest human needs, from a sense of belonging to neighborliness, stable families, meaningful work, and enlightened pursuit of self-interest.

American conservatives shared much with their liberal counterparts in this era. Central, here, was common recognition of the primary importance of private property, though over time liberals would develop ambivalence in this regard.

Whether arguing from Lockean categories or, more frequently, norms drawn from English tradition, both conservatives and liberals understood property as a moral reality, emphasizing people's moral right to their possessions in the face of governmental demands.

Another justification for private property, equally important in the founding period: protecting people's right to hold private property and use it for their own purposes binds people to a government committed to providing those protections. Propertied citizens can take care of themselves in most matters and develop both the taste and the habit for self-reliance – a necessary condition for a self-ruling people. In many ways property holders function like Aristotle's famous "middling class" by providing political prudence tied to self-interest. Private property, and the self-interest that governs the use of that property, works well to satisfy basic human needs and is useful, indeed essential, to the maintenance of civil society.

In addition, conservatives in particular emphasized that the varied forms of common law property holding – from outright ownership to leaseholds and local community ownership – enable people to engage with one another outside of government. They build relationships rooted in the exchange of goods and services. Governments must protect private property but cannot provide the social capital that self-governing property holders create through their relationships. Learning to settle trusts, create licenses and tenancies, organize businesses, and form corporations gives a free people both organizational skills and proclivities for other civil associations.

Where liberals eventually came to see private self-interest and the common good as necessarily hostile, conservatives have seen them as interdependent. Thus American conservatives did not develop the habit of seeing private and public interests as mutually incompatible, or self-reliance as antagonistic to the common good. Property relations have become more complicated as the government has fostered new forms that can be used in ways hostile to local community, but the link between property ownership and a healthy society remains central to any authentic version of American conservatism.

Critics on the left have seized on the American tradition's emphasis on private property to question the legitimacy of the most important document within that tradition, the Constitution. They portray the Constitution as "conservative" in the pejorative sense of protecting a selfish, propertied class in its ability to exploit others. On this view, any defense of the moral virtue connected with private property is but a thinly disguised defense of exploitation. These critics are partly correct but profoundly wrong. The conditions that prepared the way for a constitutional convention included a genuine fear of disorder, and among the forms of disorder were many cases in which government policies undermined the stability and value of property. In a more general way, the widespread belief, most closely associated with what would become conservatism, that liberty is always threatened when society is disordered, caused many leaders to believe that a new government capable of such ordered protection of liberties and property was necessary. Their goals were not exploitative but protective – protection of the rights of Americans and of the social fabric that sustains a free people.

We confront here one of the challenges inherent in the conservative tradition: it is not an ideology; it is not a comprehensive moral system declaring truths easily summarized in simple formulas. In essence, what we mean by conservatism begins with the identification and articulation of the moral principles we might call natural as they emerge from the living currents of history. This conservative task is never completed but rather always open to revision, and so requires prudential balancing without any claim to definitive abstract knowledge. Conservatism naturally emerges from the people's experiences and provides a natural, legitimate check on that people's passions. It emerges from Americans' lived experiences but can be grasped as guiding norms that can restrain a democratic people from radical, simplifying actions in response to bewildering, or even frightening, change.

CHAPTER THREE

Principled Conservatism
Confronting the Problem of Change

Conservatism is rooted in lived experience. Its principles are not abstractions but summaries of norms, evoking right or virtuous conduct under given circumstances. What, then, is a conservative to do when circumstances change with frightening speed or when the order one seeks to preserve includes injustices that violate first principles? Stated in general terms, the answer is fairly simple: draw on relevant examples from the past and work to address abuses while maintaining decency and ordered liberty. In practice, however, this kind of reasoning, and action, is difficult – and becomes increasingly difficult as the scope of the injustice and pace of change increase. Moreover, conservatives in such times must contend with ideologues whose simplistic "solutions" offer a compelling moralism shorn of all human complexity. The abstractly moral claim is particularly attractive in disordered times, allowing each individual to find his own purity in it. Conservatives know, however, that real life, entailing countless responses to varying circumstances, demands messy but necessary compromises precluded as much by ideological rigidity as by facile accommodation.

Like all generations, that of the American founding made mistakes, in part bound by its predecessors' immoral choices. Of these, slavery, our most un-American institution, continues to define Americans' ongoing debate about the character of our republic. As the institution most hostile to principles of self-rule and the pursuit of happiness, slavery was fundamentally inconsistent with both conservatism and liberalism, even though both conservatives and liberals at times endorsed it. In doing so, conservatives and liberals violated their own principles, often employing brilliant but tortured logic in defense of an evil from which they profited, and their moral failure damaged the integrity of both American traditions. But we cannot define either liberalism or conservatism by those episodes where they violate their own norms, nor ought we use hypocrisy to introduce deep skepticism about the stated principles of these traditions. We must reclaim the principles and norms that have emerged from our tradition, not the selfish or misguided abuses of our principles, even as we resist the siren song of hatred and resentment.

An unvarnished explanation of slavery's development in America can help us understand more general conservative principles of governance. Outright prohibition of slavery was politically impossible at the time of the Constitution's ratification, and, because the need for a Constitution was pressing, the central question concerns how the framers sought to deal with this institution short of outlawing it. Perhaps the most attractive defense was made by Abraham Lincoln, who argued from reason and textual analysis that the framers believed the Constitution helped put slavery on the path to extinction. Conditions they could not foresee thwarted their plan, leaving it to Lincoln's generation to face the problem.

We do not need to embrace Lincoln's sympathetic interpretation in order to clarify the underlying principles at work. We can, and must, acknowledge the role played by greed and by false, destructive, and un-Christian racial theories in entrenching slavery in America. Still, any reasonable assessment of relevant motives confronts a deeper truth about conservative principles. By common law, slavery was illegal. The underlying common law doctrine of "free English soil" holds that as a matter of natural justice no man who stands on English soil – including in English colonies and on English ships – can be the property of another. Sir William Blackstone, the premier mid-eighteenth-century commentator on the common law and a deeply influential thinker among colonial Americans, included the free English soil doctrine among the "absolute rights of individuals" in common law.

The clarity of this doctrine did not always translate into clarity of practice or positive law. The most persistent form of involuntary servitude in England for centuries had been "villeinage," in which a "villein" was partially free but bound to provide specified labor and to remain on the lands of his lord. This practice, almost extinct by 1600 in England, bears no direct relationship to slavery because villeins always had protections and rights as Englishmen. In England a form of semi-slavery introduced in the seventeenth century increasingly was associated with Africans obtained by the slave trade, but its legality was unclear.

Two other factors made matters more complex: the development in the middle of the seventeenth century of Parliament's power to pass laws abrogating common law rights and the unclear nature of English laws as applied to English colonies that had their own legislatures. Both Parliament's sovereignty and the power of local legislatures to adapt law to local circumstances were seen as essential aspects of self-rule. The federal nature of the British Empire put strains on English concepts of self-rule and liberties and sanctioned other forms of rule, most famously in India. But in America, the colonies' right to make their own laws allowed them to embrace slavery through positive laws violating common law. So, the introduction of slavery in the colonies and elsewhere was an innovation – an abuse – rather than a logical extension of received tradition and refined common law principles.

For conservatives the lesson is important. The dual focus on natural law as developed and expressed in principles that emerge from practice (the common law, properly understood), and the importance for self-governing people to make their own laws, often causes conflict. The practice of self-rule is necessary for ordered liberty, and the schoolhouses of American republicanism must be local governments and associations as well as state governments. However great the latitude of a self-governing people to make their own laws, they must be limited finally by the higher moral principles expressed so well in the Anglo-American tradition of common law. Indeed, the story of the innovation of English slavery ought to remind us of the need for tradition as a restraint on power. Only legal and psychological innovations "freeing" the English and Americans from tradition enabled them to introduce and then justify this specific form of barbarism. However complicated the process by which colonial Americans came to accept and employ slavery, and however apparently necessary for the social and economic order slavery had become by the founding period, it was a fundamental violation of conservative moral principles as developed empirically and historically and as reflecting colonists' understanding of natural law.

Tragically, after the Civil War finally put an end to chattel slavery, millions of freed slaves were forced into a corrupt form of villeinage due to the self-interest and fear of all too many in the white population. We take up Americans' deeply flawed attempts to address racial animosity in a later chapter. But slavery and its aftermath were only the clearest and most destructive example of societal failure in the face of change. Economic and attending social and cultural changes, on a magnitude and at a speed unknown in modern history, forged an era in which conservative principles were most needed but least self-evident. In late-nineteenth-century America the transformation in global markets, in the nature of economic production, and in the social order rooted in an agricultural and Protestant nation fostered the growth of political ideology. Conservatism sounds like nostalgia to many when they are in the midst of economic transformation and when the search for principles to order this new age do not naturally include an appeal to tradition or inherited norms.

Sometimes called the Great Divergence or the Great Enrichment, the period beginning about 1750 witnessed exponential improvements in technology in the West (primarily in Great Britain), corresponding increases in wealth, and social and economic changes that ruptured centuries of living patterns and traditions in Europe as well as more recent patterns in the United States. In the late nineteenth century these changes accelerated, bringing Americans, like the British decades before and most of the world decades later, into historical currents of change and economic progress previously unknown. In every case, dramatic material and economic progress also brought painful social dislocation, the extinction of long-established institutions, dramatic changes of power and institutional function, and, as in all periods of rapid change, a widespread feeling of fragility and insecurity in which the past seemed no guide to the near future.

Consider a few of the changes that transformed the American economy and society beginning in the later part of the nineteenth century. In this first great modern age of globalization, farmers, manufacturers, merchants, and bankers operated in markets that were vast and inexplicable. Technological advances made possible machines that could exponentially increase manufacturing efficiency, if only producers could find sufficient capital to acquire them. Global flows of capital became available, and the federal government made it easier to pool capital by enacting laws that encouraged investments while limiting liability on those investments. States like New Jersey furthered this trend with laws allowing for the creation of holding companies.

Several factors contributed to the success of this revolution: a related revolution in transportation lowered costs and increased reliability; widespread dependence on the gold standard stabilized currencies, lowering the costs and increasing the predictability of doing business outside of national borders; very low tariffs created a vast (nearly) free-trade zone. These and other factors helped make emerging manufacturing interests very attractive for international investment. The only disadvantage American manufacturing faced was a relative weakness in its labor market. American manufacturing, already well established, was dependent on skilled laborers organized into self-governing guilds. For America to compete in the global market under the new industrial system, it would need fewer skilled workers and a dramatic increase in cheap labor. The result was a surge of immigrants, mainly from poor rural regions of eastern and southern Europe, which lowered industrial wages and forced out many skilled workers, creating a new cultural mix in many large cities.

Changes brought about during this period challenged deeply held conservative beliefs and required a rethinking of the relationship between principle and context. The challenge was great not only because of the speed of change but because rapid economic and social transformations present a much greater intellectual challenge than does political revolution: these transformations alter the very experiences of daily life from which cultural norms emerge. The temptation to embrace ideology over principle intensifies when the world one inhabits is no longer familiar. With few ideologies at hand in America, European ideas percolated in the United States for the first time, usually among immigrants. Various forms of socialism offered answers to the alienation of the period, though these answers were not well connected to the American experience. Eventually an American ideology (influenced by Europeans but truly American) emerged on the left in the first decades of the twentieth century. That ideology was called progressivism. Conservatism, meanwhile, fell into a state of confusion because its adherents could not respond quickly under such conditions, nor did the underlying conditions appear stable or durable enough to ensure continuity. No two generations shared the same social or cultural context.

Conservative and liberal principles, to say nothing of certain elements of leftist ideologies, mixed in complex ways during this era. Outside of the essentially European ideologies that gave loud but marginalized voice to the problem, Americans responded out of very specific self-interests and in ways intended to preserve self-rule. An important example is the farmers' revolt we label "populism." Farmers were quintessentially self-reliant Americans. But during this era they were caught in a new global system in which the price of agricultural products went down, even as a monopolistic railroad system kept costs high and an international monetary system produced periods of deflation along with constriction of available credit. Farmers felt betrayed by elites who controlled global markets. In a predictable pattern of reaction, they began by trying to organize and work together to solve their problems but eventually turned to political action, demanding government assistance to bring fairness to the system and allow farmers to return to self-reliance in the new globalized marketplace.

A wide variety of reactions developed elsewhere. Members of the rising professional classes worked to professionalize and bring order to municipal governments. Local elites sought to Americanize a bewildering array of new immigrants through government schools. Some progressive urbanites even sought government regulations to ensure the safety of trolleys they did not build and food they did not grow. The common denominator was an attempt to create order while responding to the loss of the conditions for self-reliance. The same can be said of the growing union movement that sought self-empowerment to ensure security and higher wages. In culture, morals, and religion, a similar urge for stability produced a Victorianism that sought to preserve received tastes and values in an economy and social order in which both were dissolved into preference and desire; Darwinism and ideologized criticism (e.g., socialism and anarchism) prompted fundamentalism in response to what were seen as intellectual threats. As conservatives sought to find their footing, a plethora of movements and demands seemed to create ever more uncertainty, along with a drive toward ideology and state action as tools for making sense of seeming disorder.

Conservative principles were not destroyed during this time of confusion. But conservative thought was in turmoil. Henry Adams, among the greatest thinkers in the American tradition, saw the conflict between conservative norms and material reality and responded with a spiritual hopelessness that was, for all its brilliance, debilitating. Politicians and judges seemed to fall into one of two camps: those who provided uncritical support for large-scale organizations that hid their reliance on the state behind a myth of laissez-faire, and those who expressed revulsion at economic dislocation, ignored real increases in material wealth, and demanded ever more political control over people's lives. There were exceptions, however. Ironically it was the Catholic convert Orestes Brownson who, writing soon after the Civil War, best captured the continuing principles of the American republic. Insisting that the fundamentally Protestant American founding was rooted in the tradition of natural law, Brownson affirmed the reality of our equality in the sight of God, our possession of important rights, and our natural limitations. He also affirmed the necessity of local self-rule, which he termed "territorial democracy," and the reality of an unwritten constitution of traditions, customs, and beliefs residing in the people whose "sovereign power" constitutes the nation. As Brownson put it in his book *The American Republic*, published in 1865, this unwritten constitution "is Providential, not made by the nation, but born with it. The written constitution is made and ordained by the sovereign power, and presupposes that power as already existing and constituted."*

This unwritten constitution continued to exist during the late nineteenth century. The people had covenanted themselves into a republic, founded on natural law principles and dedicated to self-rule and the pursuit of happiness under God. But conservatives were tasked with the duty of applying that unwritten constitution in times of radical economic change that were transforming social and cultural norms. In particular, they had a duty to ask how the new economic order had refined the meaning of private property. If the sanctity of private prop-

---

* Orestes A. Brownson, *The American Republic: Its Constitution, Tendencies, and Destiny* (Wilmington, DE: ISI Books, 2003), 122.

erty is central to the meaning and ideals of American conservatism, it is also true that the nature and uses of property were changing profoundly. New government protections for corporate investment encouraged colossal concentrations of capital that existed solely for the purpose of making a profit – and did nothing to serve communal interests, even if politicians like Theodore Roosevelt wanted to harness them for national interests. The advantages of this development in property were obvious in a global economy, but less obvious were deeper concerns about how property had conventionally served to connect people in community and how property, including investment property, had long been attached to more specific economic purposes: adding acreage to the ranch, building a new store, pooling money to start a business in a community.

The fact that investment property flooded the American economy from all over the world signaled a change in the meaning and purpose of property, but without a clear conservative principle to guide this expanded meaning. American conservatism has yet to well articulate a revised defense of private property in line with the goods that it ought to serve. During the early twentieth century this failure would leave the American tradition vulnerable to massive shifts in ideology and power.

CHAPTER FOUR

Alternative Visions
Conservatism Meets Progressivism and the New Deal

The rise of ideology in late-nineteenth-century America presented challenges beyond those inherent in the political, economic, and cultural changes of the time. By the early twentieth century, progressivism had become a powerful force – a movement declaring that the structures and limitations of the American Constitution must be set aside so that "the people's will" could be divined and put into action by a centralized federal government in an era of centralized national and international economic power. While conservatives entered into a complex and sustained engagement with these challenges, conservative prejudices, habits, and norms remained strong in America, thriving in New England, the Midwest, the Great Plains, the Mountain West, and, in an eccentric version, in the South. In these regions, communities were organized around the principles of ordered liberty in the context of community and reciprocity among neighbors. There the people belonged to myriad voluntary and fraternal associations, they stressed biblical religion, and they continued to believe in the centrality of self-reliance.

From this stream of practical American conservatism came one of the key figures in this tradition: Calvin Coolidge. Coolidge gave conservatism a spare but eloquent voice, enlivening coherent principles and norms in a time of change. He grew up in New England, one of the seedbeds of local self-rule, rooted in a culture dedicated to both thick community and the self-reliance of individuals and families. Educated classically at Amherst College, Coolidge came of age with a deep knowledge of, and love for, American history, and he drew special inspiration from Abraham Lincoln. As a young lawyer (among the few by his time to still enter that profession through apprenticeship rather than attending law school), Coolidge often defended the property rights of small interests. While he understood the importance of concentrations of capital, he stressed that work was prior to capital and that ordered liberty rests on the ability of people to use their freedom and their labor to create property and supply the necessary conditions of life in self-governing associations.

Throughout his career's ascent from local politics to governor of Massachusetts and ultimately president of the United States, Coolidge embodied the conservative politician as have few others. He was deeply rooted in his regional culture, devoted to his family and the range of obligations that make family important to each person's identity, hard-working and self-reliant, intensely patriotic, quietly but profoundly religious, and committed to the principles of conservatism while offering no ideology. In times of dramatic change, Coolidge sought to apply conservative principles.

A practical but passionate focus on freedom and opportunity shaped Coolidge's prudential response to progressive reforms. Devoted to constitutionalism and fully aware of society's reliance on deep, widespread respect for the law, Coolidge generally accepted reforms done within the limits of both. When Theodore Roosevelt used the Sherman Anti-Trust Act of 1890 to break up monopolies, Coolidge appreciated this government action designed to provide greater opportunities for entrepreneurs and small commercial interests. Here Roosevelt acted within the law and did so in defense of what Coolidge called the American ideal. In his many local and state roles, including mayor and governor, Coolidge not only worked to prevent monopolies from taking away opportunities but also followed Roosevelt's lead in trying to find common ground between labor unions and corporations.

Coolidge sought to encourage economic and technological progress in ways that supported communal self-governance. The railroads, primary targets of progressive reformers, for Coolidge were crucial assets for communities. To deliver its services a railroad needed huge amounts of capital and certain governmental protections. But only the railroads, even within certain inescapable regional monopolies, allowed small towns easy access to larger cities and markets. In this case, a well-run and properly regulated, relatively corruption-free railroad supported both economic growth and self-governing local communities.

Accepting some of its reforms, Coolidge opposed progressivism's ideology. This opposition emerged in response to the administration of President Woodrow Wilson and particularly its actions during World War I. The federal government, under the guise of wartime measures, had violated many sacred American principles. The Wilson administration had abused property rights, undermined constitutional limitations on federal power embodied in the Tenth Amendment and the structures of federalism, and expanded presidential powers through unconstitutional executive actions. Worse yet, the Wilson administration undertook the most extensive repression of speech and civil liberties in American history, imprisoning and deporting thousands without due process for any speech the government deemed subversive, including any "abusive language" against the flag, the Constitution, and American military uniforms. These wartime measures built on years of abuses – including Wilson's personal decision to impose racial segregation among federal employees – and exposed the power of an imperial presidency to rule without law.

The authoritarian and lawless nature of the progressive regime frightened Coolidge and set the context for the policies and practices he would pursue as president. Coolidge believed that his primary task as president was to manage the government well, according to the strict requirements of law and the Constitution. Thus he devoted much of his energy not to introducing changes but to making the government responsive within its limited realm. After a spate of progressive reforms (many salutary and legal, but many others harmful to American principles and extralegal), Coolidge wanted government to get out of the way of self-reliant Americans while working efficiently to create and sustain the order and structure that facilitated private and associational life.

Coolidge's learned and brilliant speech celebrating the 150th anniversary of the Declaration of Independence articulated American principles as well as any presidential address. Rejecting the progressive claim that the Constitution was an open-ended call for ceaseless change in the name of personal autonomy, Coolidge insisted that the American revolutionaries were no radicals. Rather, the Revolution "was conservative and represented the action of the colonists to maintain their constitutional rights which from time immemorial had been guaranteed to them under the law of the land."* Coolidge deftly

---

* Calvin Coolidge, "Address at the Celebration of the 150th Anniversary of the Declaration of Independence in Philadelphia, Pennsylvania," July 5, 1926. *The American Presidency Project*, Gerhard Peters and John T. Woolley, eds., https://www. presidency.ucsb.edu/node/267359.

explored the deep religious sources of American principles while connecting "natural rights" to both these religious commitments and the Anglo-American tradition.

In a speech welcoming Charles Lindbergh back to America and celebrating his famous solo flight across the Atlantic, Coolidge articulated the principles most evident to American conservatives in this time. First, he praised Lindbergh's character. For conservatives, character had long been a key term denoting a well-formed person: one who has matured so as to be self-governing, in mastery of his passions, and in love with good and noble things, and who possesses such virtues as to be a good citizen, family member, and neighbor. To praise a man's character is to suggest that he is unspoiled, unwilling to "commercialize" himself or to seek cheap fame. More than that, to praise a man's character implies praise of his family, his community, and those who helped form him. And so Coolidge gave clear voice to the conservative view of the self-reliant man – one with character, shaped by others in tandem with his own indomitable will to become self-possessed and self-ruling. Moreover, the liberty of the individual person is possible only when the relevant social institutions have shaped that person to possess good character. Otherwise liberty is transmuted into libidinous license, which ends not in self-rule but in a pathetic form of dependence.

Coolidge did not confine himself to praise for Lindbergh; he made special mention of the more than one hundred American companies that contributed to the making of Lindbergh's plane. It was a technological marvel, and it would not have been possible without the "genius" of American economic liberty. Coolidge called these companies "silent partners" with Lindbergh and praised American economic ingenuity because America's free-market system, when it is entrepreneurial, helps empower people of character, of strong will and desire, to make their mark on the world. The American hero – as exemplified by the brave, solitary pilot – is possible only through community and by way of American principles at work in the economy and society. Conspicuously, Coolidge celebrated Lindbergh's achievement as a sign of American greatness: a greatness not made by government action but arising out of its people and their sense of industry.

Coolidge embraced prudential reforms labeled "progressive" when they served American communities, traditions, and principles. He opposed ideological progressivism, which focuses on the abstract idea of a "good society" while pursuing particular goods in defiance of constitutional and historical norms and regardless of social costs. This progressivism would come to dominate the American government during the New Deal and the war years that followed. Because progressives believed that modern conditions had made inherited constitutionalism obsolete, they helped construct a different purpose for the federal government. During the New Deal and its aftermath, a government claiming to guarantee the substantive good of the people also claimed unprecedented power to do so. Conservatives thus confronted a challenge new both in principle and in degree. This confrontation would help spawn the modern conservative movement. The great American conversation was no longer limited to American liberals and conservatives; a new species of progressive liberalism (a version of leftism) would become important in shaping the America of the next hundred years. The most powerful figure in writing this progressive ideology into American politics was Franklin Delano Roosevelt.

FDR's pedigree and character did not suit him ideally for the role of revolutionary. Inheritor of vast wealth and privilege, holder of no particular deep thoughts or convictions, he forged his "New Deal" out of expediency and short-term responses to great events. Consequently, if Roosevelt's New Deal was not doctrinaire progressivism, the regime clearly had no sense of loyalty to inherited principles. His presidency and the New Deal represented experimentation with new powers and new methods, and this alone made them dangerous. Vastly expanding work begun under Wilson, the Roosevelt presidency presented American conservatives not only with ideological challenges but also with a vastly expanded federal government, with new powers and new institutions that would be almost impossible to reverse. This, along with new geopolitical realities during World War II and the subsequent Cold War, produced novel conditions for American conservatives and required compromises, coalitions, and challenging decisions about which principles must be preserved and which ones might be temporarily sacrificed to the exigencies of the historical moment. These factors produced a movement that included powerful conservative voices but embraced a competing liberal ideology: a right-wing liberalism. This modern conservative movement could function only so long as the conditions that produced it were still operative. But if this new movement would not be fully conservative, it nonetheless represented the most prudent option for conservatives during times of unprecedented challenges to individual liberties and the nation as a whole.

The New Deal rested on assumptions and declarations that deviated from the American tradition and became more radical over time. First, as declared in his famous Commonwealth Address, Roosevelt believed that the principles and forms of government established in the founding were outdated. Second, the New Deal assumed that modern life required of the federal government a level of involvement in regulation and support formerly unknown in the United States and inconsistent with constitutional limitations. Third, even more than Wilson, FDR built a bureaucracy premised on belief that the complexity of the circumstances combined with the new roles played by government required experts to make decisions outside the democratic process. The Roosevelt administration did dramatically more than any prior administration to turn governance over to a managerial class of bureaucratic elites and academic advisors. Fourth, because of the New Deal the new capitalism was going to be steered less by entrepreneurs and more by the joint efforts of business and government managers. Fifth, the Roosevelt administration established the enduring principle that the federal government has a compelling interest in providing basic protections for its citizens, from old-age pensions to direct and indirect assistance to find work or obtain unemployment support.

The sixth change, which came at the hands of the Supreme Court, is perhaps the most important. In a dramatic reversal in constitutional interpretation, the Supreme Court authorized Congress to make laws, establish agencies, and create new powers as it wished so long as these changes served the "general welfare" of the American people. The key passage in the Constitution is found in Article I, Section 8: "The Congress shall have power to lay and collect taxes, ... to pay the debts and provide for the common defense and general welfare of the United States." Since the founding period, this section had been understood as a limit on the "enumerated powers" of Congress. In effect, it outlines the specific powers delegated to Congress and states that, outside of those specifically enumerated, Congress has no authority. For the Constitution's framers, the general welfare language further limits the power of Congress by saying that legislators could use the enumerated powers only to the degree that they were providing for the general welfare. It was out of an abundance of caution that the First Congress proposed what would become the Tenth Amendment to the Constitution, specifically stating that "the powers not delegated to the United States by the Constitution, nor prohibited by it to the States, are reserved to the States respectively, or to the people." No major Supreme Court decision and no real precedent existed for a different understanding of the constitutional language until the Supreme Court's 1937 decision in *Helvering v. Davis*, along with several subsequent decisions over the next five years.

Without any democratic process, and without any developed precedent, the Supreme Court handed Congress the power to do whatever its members deemed in the general welfare, expanding the reach and power of the federal government beyond anything imagined at the founding or chosen by the people. The contrast with earlier progressive reforms is important: to accomplish their key goals, progressives followed the constitutional amendment process to alter that document four times in seven years. Since that time, armed with a handful of unelected judges' novel interpretation of the general welfare clause, Congress, presidents and executive agencies, and even courts repeatedly have increased the power and reach of the federal government without recourse to the constitutional amendment process. This broadened understanding of federal power as tending to the needs of the people has undermined the people's formerly cherished principle of self-reliance.

Strangely neglected in discussions about preserving constitutional rule, the *Helvering* decision undermines two essential principles of Anglo-American conservatism, that governments must be limited in their scope of power and that only the people have the authority to grant powers. Once congressional power extends to anything it deems relevant to the citizens' welfare, limits on governmental power become unclear and may change with congressional or judicial whim. Worse yet, this expansion of congressional power alters the nature of the relationship between the executive and legislative branches. Congress, passing laws to assist in the general welfare, turns over the administration of those laws to the executive branch. The modern president directs and oversees a vast administrative system, giving the executive branch near-complete freedom, subject primarily to checks from the judiciary, to determine how to administer the laws. Congress might pass a law requiring clean air, for example, but it is an administrative agency, which answers to the president but not to the people, that defines clean air, determines what regulations must be in place to achieve clean air, and decides how to enforce regulations the agency itself interprets. Congress ends by abdicating most of its newfound power to an ever more imperial presidency.

No sustained American conservatism – no ordered liberty, no rule of law, and certainly no respect for traditions of self-governing communities – is possible without altering this power arrangement and without establishing clear boundaries and checks on power. A large, powerful, distant government wars against the conditions that foster self-rule and attachment to institutions that ought to connect individuals to their society and their nation. We can expect no truly conservative political regime unless we reclaim the robust power of the people to authorize and limit what governments can do and by what means. If we can understand that the conditions of World War II and the Cold War might have prevented conservatives from giving appropriate attention to this abuse of constitutional powers, we can insist that the time to reclaim our protections against tyranny is now.

Even before World War II, the Roosevelt administration had put in place a set of principles and practices hostile to American constitutional traditions. The reception of these changes, however, was complicated and would shape the coming conservative movement in profound ways. Conservative responses to FDR's innovations were vigorous and numerous. But among those who grew up during the Depression, their understanding of the New Deal was emotionally complex. Many, like Ronald Reagan, would be critical of certain parts of the New Deal but otherwise see in FDR and his policies a genuine effort to empower the "forgotten man" – to help him, with a job and a safety net, to regain the dignity of being able to take care of himself and his family without "going on the dole." By the same token, the often forgotten pressures of a life-and-death struggle with Marxist totalitarianism during the Cold War caused most Americans to overlook or accept the ever-solidifying concentration of federal government power in the interests of victory in a long, difficult, and often bloody international struggle. It is to these post–World War II realities that we turn next.

CHAPTER FIVE

The New Conservatism and the Cold War

The World War II generation went through a crushing economic depression followed by a global war of massive
destruction. Many had looked to government to save them
from desolation, and to help them maintain their dignity by
giving them jobs rather than handouts. This generation had
witnessed the power of government to defeat both Imperial
Japan and Nazi Germany, freeing much of the world from
shocking brutality and tyranny. Of all American generations,
those who came of age in the 1940s developed the deepest
trust in government and its ability to serve the general welfare.
And so, as the war ended, they continued to trust their government as it faced new challenges from international communism, and to enjoy the benefits they saw coming from its
expanded role in economic life. While President Harry Truman
failed to expand as much as he had hoped on the New Deal,
President Dwight Eisenhower showed little interest in disman-
tling the government that FDR's administrators had cobbled
together.

In this atmosphere the conservative movement coalesced
during the 1950s and gained political steam in the period from
the 1960s through the 1980s. In this endeavor conservatives
faced a complex interplay between, on one hand, principles of
federalism and rugged individualism, and, on the other, general

acceptance of the national government as master of a massive military and intelligence apparatus and massive programs aimed at protecting vulnerable people. Conservatism was more or less forced to operate within the New Deal paradigm.

Most Americans supported New Deal–type programs for the understandable reason that they benefited from them. The education benefits and low-cost mortgages and loans offered by the GI Bill allowed hundreds of thousands of veterans to become property-owning members of the middle class. As important, the government-business partnership during the war had produced an industrial base beyond anything previously imagined. Untouched by the destruction of war, this base propelled America to economic supremacy in the postwar era. For this generation, then, economic success, combined with America's geopolitical dominance, gave ample proof that the American way of life was the happy result of large government and industrial capitalism working together for the general welfare.

Subsequent events would show how short-lived and ultimately self-defeating New Deal policies really were. But problems of social breakdown, welfare dependency, imperial overreach, and cultural malaise did not become undeniably concrete and obvious until the 1970s. Meanwhile, after the Allied victory in 1945, America moved from global war into a decades-long standoff with the Soviet Union. Major wars inevitably centralize power, and the Cold War was no exception; extending the crises of World War II, it altered the American military, economy, politics, and, most important of all, culture, undermining the conditions necessary for the flourishing of a self-governing people.

Sustained confrontation with the Soviet Union required the United States to take on global military and treaty commitments and to construct a huge, unprecedented surveillance system to spy on enemies and to work in secret to keep the nation safe. This Cold War required an ongoing and symbiotic relationship between the military-security establishment, key industries, and research facilities providing the United States with its strategic advantage in technology.

The Cold War also effectively split the world in two, preventing a return to globalism. In the dichotomy between the free world and the Soviet-controlled communist realm, American industry had huge competitive advantages, gaining dominance for the next several decades. In addition, Cold War demands for more innovation, technology, and consumer goods (the last to prove our material superiority) supported a social order widely referred to as the American way of life. Secure in the nation's economic dominance, management cooperated with labor, giving workers an increasing standard of living for the next several decades. More ominously, Americans largely came to accept the central role played by experts and the managerial class, both in government and in large corporations.

Casting a shadow over all these developments was an existential threat that altered all public discourse, sharply limiting the range of political positions Americans could tolerate. Nuclear holocaust was a realistic possibility as the arms race accelerated and America faced an enemy that was categorical in its assertion that it would bury us and our way of life. The Cold War was fought at many levels against an enemy using subterfuge and infiltration as well as proxy wars and threats of open violence. For these reasons, both liberals and conservatives agreed that defeating the Soviets was our most pressing national priority.

Progressives found themselves sidelined temporarily from the center of American power by their reluctance to wage the Cold War, but, as we discuss below, they expanded their influence within liberalism until, during the 1960s, they came to replace it with their own ideology. Meanwhile, liberals sustained an ardent defense of the new America that had emerged since the 1930s – a nation ruled more by elites and the managerial class, with government and business cooperating to produce a more just and equitable society. After fighting Nazism and Fascism, these liberals understood the threat posed by a totalitarian nation, particularly such a nation with nuclear arms. They therefore embraced the notion that the United States must play a dominant role in checking the Soviets and extending the reach of democracy as far as possible.

Cold War liberals were aided in their drive to justify the new welfare-warfare state by their commitment to the ideals of freedom and equality and the belief that these ideals could be realized in a managed society and economy. Many conservatives, eschewing such a rationalization, steadfastly argued against the New Deal paradigm and the rise of the security state. Most, however, accepted that the United States must maintain a large, sophisticated military, though they rejected the call for America to become a redeemer nation spreading democracy. These reluctant conservative cold warriors were suspicious of entangling alliances like NATO (usually for constitutional reasons) but agreed that the Soviet threat was real and required new positioning in international politics.

Conservatives had the advantage of basing their arguments on principles rooted in the American experience. They struggled, however, to offer a persuasive argument about how vigorous opposition to the Soviets could be reconciled with the American tradition. New, dangerous, and unprecedented conditions required conservative reassessment.

Over the course of the 1950s a new conservatism emerged. At first this "movement" was little more than a loose collection of influential books written in reaction to frightening conditions, each speaking in its own voice. It included Russell Kirk's brilliant *The Conservative Mind*, a volume published in 1953 that reclaimed an intellectual patrimony emerging from Edmund Burke, carrying through to the Spanish-American philosopher George Santayana and, later, the American-born English poet-philosopher T. S. Eliot. At times idiosyncratic, the book was a masterpiece of historical mythmaking. Even as Western civilization seemed in the throes of cultural suicide and America was transforming itself in a statist mold, Kirk's story of historical continuities connected with an unexpectedly large audience hungry for a steadfast American devotion to the highest and most enduring principles. Seen from a certain perspective, this account gave America a historic opportunity to save Western civilization from itself – a role we might hope Americans embrace with renewed fervor today.

Robert Nisbet responded to the destruction of the institutions that had given meaning, structure, and purpose to people's lives. Also published in 1953, *The Quest for Community* noted that the desire for community was a universal part of the human condition. The question is not whether we will have community but whether we will have healthy community. We will either have the rich associational life of free and self-ruling people described so well by Tocqueville or we will be seduced into surrendering ourselves to an all-encompassing ersatz community of the state.

Richard Weaver, in his arresting *Ideas Have Consequences*, published in 1948, offered an eccentric but powerful defense of essences – the assertion that there are truths and forms that are not products of will or choice but are in the nature of things. His complex defense of universal truths (a natural law vision long attacked by intellectual forces in America and Europe) was wrapped in a defense of southern agrarianism that stressed the necessity of rootedness, a deep historical culture, and tradition. With Weaver we find the conservative mind trying to resolve its defining tension between transcendent truths and historicism.

Friedrich Hayek, an economist of the Austrian School whose best-known work, *The Road to Serfdom*, was published in Britain in 1944, offered a stirring defense of individualism and freedom against statism, the managerial class, and various forms of hidden collectivism. Other Europeans hit similar themes that connected with American audiences, suggesting that their experiences and analyses, drawn from decades of European decadence, made them particularly aware of the deep and seductive dangers of creeping socialism and the allure of national community. These Europeans believed they had something to teach Americans, and many Americans were willing to learn.

These new conservatives shared the conviction that Soviet communism posed the greatest threat to their most cherished principles. More controversial was the nature of these principles and the internal danger to them. Unlike liberals, almost all of the new conservatives accepted that liberty or freedom was more important than equality, especially because "equality" had come to mean not the striving for equality of opportunity but the imposition by a class of managers of policies aimed at equalizing outcomes. All these conservatives struggled with thorny questions about how to fight for ordered liberty and self-rule while also supporting a nation engaged in an ongoing war requiring state power and reach that no previous conservative would have endorsed.

Perhaps the best statement of truly conservative principles in this context emerged from the founding of the student group Young Americans for Freedom in 1960. Named the Sharon Statement and crafted at the home of the new conservatives' chief spokesman and binding force, William F. Buckley Jr., it is worth quoting in full:

> *In this time of moral and political crises, it is the responsibility of the youth of America to affirm certain eternal truths.*
>
> *We, as young conservatives, believe:*
>
> *That foremost among the transcendent values is the individual's use of his God-given free will, whence derives his right to be free from the restrictions of arbitrary force;*
>
> *That liberty is indivisible, and that political freedom cannot long exist without economic freedom;*
>
> *That the purpose of government is to protect those freedoms through the preservation of internal order, the provision of national defense, and the administration of justice;*
>
> *That when government ventures beyond these rightful functions, it accumulates power, which tends to diminish order and liberty;*
>
> *That the Constitution of the United States is the best arrangement yet devised for empowering government to fulfill its proper role, while restraining it from the concentration and abuse of power;*
>
> *That the genius of the Constitution – the division of powers – is summed up in the clause that reserves primacy to the several states, or to the people, in those spheres not specifically delegated to the Federal government;*
>
> *That the market economy, allocating resources by the free play of supply and demand, is the single economic system compatible with the requirements of personal freedom and constitutional government, and that it is at the same time the most productive supplier of human needs;*
>
> *That when government interferes with the work of the market economy, it tends to reduce the moral and physical strength*

of the nation; that when it takes from one man to bestow on another, it diminishes the incentive of the first, the integrity of the second, and the moral autonomy of both;

That we will be free only so long as the national sovereignty of the United States is secure; that history shows periods of freedom are rare, and can exist only when free citizens concertedly defend their rights against all enemies;

That the forces of international Communism are, at present, the greatest single threat to these liberties;

That the United States should stress victory over, rather than coexistence with, this menace; and

That American foreign policy must be judged by this criterion: does it serve the just interests of the United States?*

This document expresses most every theme that had evolved in American conservatism. It also lays out why the nation's foreign policy must respond to communism. It is conservatism in response to the realities of the Cold War.

The Sharon Statement begins with an affirmation of transcendent truths and follows with a list of beliefs that have emerged out of the English and, later, American traditions of self-rule. It is as redolent of English principles of common law, principles of limited government, inherited liberty, and rights of property as anything John Adams wrote. The statement both challenges the rise of liberal government interference in the economy and outlines the moral imperative to defeat communism. The closing sentence presents interesting challenges for later members of the conservative movement. If American foreign policy is judged only by how it serves the "just interests of the

---

* Sharon Statement, adopted by Young Americans for Freedom, September 11, 1960, https://www.yaf.org/wp-content/uploads/2016/06/Sharon-Statement-1.pdf.

United States," much depends on how those interests are defined. Differences over such definitions roil conservatism to this day.

Unity never was the new conservatives' strong suit. America in the 1950s and early 1960s was thick with people attacking statism – from Ayn Rand and her followers' promoting eccentric egoism, to southerners fighting to defend local rule, to traditionalists trying to preserve their rich social order from the invading reach of government, to a wide variety of anticommunists. The early conservative movement was a rich conversation tied to a shared animus against dependence on the state. Excepting Rand's species of libertarianism, most of the voices in this conversation could speak meaningfully to others without needing to find agreement. But the need for consensus becomes more pressing when one wants to organize a political movement. The primary means by which this movement began to take shape was Buckley's journal of opinion, *National Review*, which began publication in 1955.

National Review's mission statement captured well the conservative movement's challenges. Why, Buckley asked, in a "conservative" nation do we need a conservative journal of opinion? He believed the nation was truly conservative in the same way Coolidge did – the people are deeply rooted in families and communities and love their nation, their culture, and their intellectual inheritance. The problem, then, is not with the people. The problem is that "literate America rejected conservatism in favor of radical social experimentation." "Literate" here is code for academia and the arbiters of culture and taste among elite institutions. These people, progressives with increasing influence on liberal groups and policies, rejected the traditions and the metaphysical premises that had governed Americans for centuries; they undermined ordered liberty, seeking to transform America according to a progressive utopian vision.

The most famous line of Buckley's essay is the declaration that *National Review* "stands athwart history, yelling Stop."** Buckley declares *National Review* to be an intellectual journal in defense of our cultural, intellectual, and constitutional heritage against those who seek to chart a new future – an arc of history designed by those who reject tradition. In short, *National Review* is engaging in battle with the intellectual establishment for the future of America, defending a conservative people against the progressive elites who despise their way of life and their very character.

National Review did not produce uniformity of thought. It brought together an eclectic group of thinkers, and many arguments raged within its pages. But these thinkers' common goals were clear, and it was their dedication to shared principles that made the magazine the most important guiding institution in the early years of the conservative movement. It was through *National Review* that the boundaries of acceptable positions were defined. The John Birch Society and Ayn Rand were sent to the hinterlands. Traditionalists like Kirk were placed in uncomfortable but respectable positions on the edges. A center – a realm of respectable intellectual and eventually political conservatism, in short, a movement – was established.

The most important battle within *National Review* during these formative years raged between "traditionalists" and "libertarians." The species of libertarians represented by Frank Meyer – *National Review* book review editor and a polemicist of the first order – understood themselves to be continuing in the American liberal tradition. As classical liberals, they parted com-

---

** William F. Buckley Jr., "Our Mission Statement," *National Review*, November 19, 1955, https://www.nationalreview.com/1955/11/our-mission-statement-william-f-buckley-jr/.

pany with the socialist tendencies of mainstream liberalism (and progressivism). Yet libertarians endorsed many of early liberalism's key principles, including the Lockean understanding of property as a natural right and the view of government as a contract. Deeply influenced by John Stuart Mill, Meyer focused on freedom and individualism as the defining goods of a society.

The traditionalists, represented by Kirk, were truer to the American conservative tradition that had emerged from English common law and extended to Calvin Coolidge. Rather than making a fetish of the sovereign individual and its radical freedom to choose as it wishes (throughout we use "it" in reference to "individual" in keeping with Kirk's and other critics' view that the individual, so conceived, is not fully human), traditionalists concentrated on the cultural, institutional, communal, religious, and legal-governmental structures necessary for ordered liberty – for the person of character so important to Coolidge. If libertarians were distinguished for their simple, appealing moral declarations, traditionalists had a more comprehensive understanding of human nature and the various structures suited to that nature.

The libertarian-traditionalist divide was the earliest cleavage in the conservative movement and perhaps reveals better than others that the new conservatism was a coalition of anti-statists rather than an uncomplicated continuation of the Anglo-American conservative tradition. Libertarian ideology is an extremely useful moral hammer when one needs to condemn injustice and declare one's own purity. But traditionalism is closer to the historically rooted social character of the people, a social character that comes to conceptual clarity only when it is threatened.

As the movement's intellectual side matured, it was riven increasingly by competing arguments and visions, almost all of them papered over with the label "conservative." Even before the influence of pro-statist, pro-interventionist neoconservatives in the 1970s, vigorous debates over the nature of the American regime and how best to understand American history produced more intricate patterns of intellectual relationships than anything American conservatism had known before.

Perhaps fittingly, the most violent and consequential battles within the conservative movement were waged over history. The argument was largely about America's origins and their meaning, about the character of the American tradition. Some saw in the American founding the distilled wisdom of the ancients, a modern bulwark against the corrosive forces of modernity that undermined virtue, truth, and natural rights. Some insisted on the peculiarly American sources of the founding, disconnecting the nation from any meaningful reliance on pre-American traditions. Others insisted on a deep communalism, rooted in small, self-governing localities threatened by modern industrialism and federal power. Savage intellectual battles raged about Lincoln's place in the American story and about the peculiar nature of the South and its history of slavery and Jim Crow.

Over time, tradition and localism increasingly were identified, almost always unfairly, with oppressive institutions and evil actions from American history. The conservative movement increasingly embraced a simple-minded reading of history as the rise of liberty and the victory of the individual over oppressive institutions. The voice of traditionalism was not silenced, even after the deaths of Kirk and Nisbet. But, in part because ideological arguments are easier to use in the rough-and-tumble of political debate and in part because progressivism in the 1960s and 1970s further undermined respect for our heritage, the conservative movement itself took on a liberal character. As we argue in the next chapter, this vision had its successes, especially when it remained connected to deeper traditions. But subsequent events would show the dangers of such a shallow understanding of America and its people.

CHAPTER SIX

Reagan and the Conservative Movement
Global Victory and Its Limits

People tend to see the history of the conservative movement as a story of rise and fall, with the presidency of
Ronald Reagan as its height. Yet, despite his many real strengths
and accomplishments, it is important to note that Reagan and
the movement that helped bring him to power were conservative in only a limited sense, and that their connection with traditionalism was muted and tangential. The conservative
movement rose to prominence in America as national politics
faced radicalism at home and abroad, as domestic politics
moved decidedly in a progressive direction, and as the postwar
boom gave way to economic stagnation. These forces pulled
the movement away from its roots in pursuit of electoral victory and power.

From the beginning, the battle over ideas within the conservative movement was important in crafting a political program
governed by principles. Translating intellectual arguments into
a political platform is by nature difficult, as the drive for electoral success encourages formulation of principles that appear
axiomatic and are easily deployed as slogans. As important, a
potent political brew of partisans, lacking any reference to the
movement's ideas, let alone conservative principles, joined during the 1960s and 1970s and proved adept at garnering power

and influence. Long before the 1990s, the conservative movement had in reality become a right-wing liberal movement that included conservatives.

There was no conservative party during the 1950s, though the Republican Party had significant conservative influences. Buckley and others sought to give the party a sharper focus and agenda, offering people what the conservative activist Phyllis Schlafly called, as the title of her 1964 book put it, "a choice not an echo." That year the Republican Party did offer a choice. Barry Goldwater's victory over Nelson Rockefeller, the standard-bearer of the party's liberal wing, to become the presidential nominee made for an ideas-driven general election against President Lyndon B. Johnson. Goldwater, an Arizona senator, picked up most of the salient themes that had emerged in the pages of *National Review*, giving them a Western, almost cowboy, libertarian hue.

Offering the most thorough critique of liberal government (including the New Deal) by any major candidate to this point, Goldwater called for an America of individualists, free to live on their own terms without government interference. He wanted the relationship between the states and the federal government to return to a stricter adherence to the founders' concept of federalism, and he offered a forceful argument for an America dedicated to the destruction of worldwide communism. An antistatist at home, he saw no conflict with a vast government effort to defeat an ideological and military enemy.

Although Goldwater was crushed in the general election, his defeat did not portend, as some predicted, the conservative movement's political collapse. Poorly organized, his campaign nevertheless galvanized idealistic young conservatives to fight for the America that Goldwater championed. A great many young Goldwater supporters chose a life of political activism, often at the state level. And, as the radical disruptions of the 1960s increased in frequency and severity, Americans concerned to protect their traditions took notice.

In the wake of the Goldwater loss, numerous demographic changes disrupted older political patterns. The rise of an evangelical Christian middle class helped produce a conservative stronghold in Southern California and fueled the rise of an emerging national political force. In the Southwest more generally, a culture that admired the self-made man, with particular emphasis on the virtue of building a business without the aid of government or corporate investment, fostered a species of libertarianism and evangelicalism that would deeply affect Ronald Reagan.

Also, of the six states that voted for Goldwater, five were in the South. No Republican had previously had such success in the South, suggesting a shift in coalitions that would alter American politics. Solidly Democratic since before the Civil War, the South had been the most reliable block of voters in the New Deal coalition that survived, in weakened form, until the 1970s. Southern hatred for the Republican Party – the party of Lincoln – would give way, in one generation, to solid support. This shift of southern whites to the Republican Party created new tensions, both in the party and in the movement.

For conservatives, the South presented a problem. No part of the nation was more dedicated to tradition, community, and local and state power, and these had long been central to conservatism. But, as we noted earlier, slavery, an institution the South had insisted on perpetuating to the point of civil war, was an obvious violation of received tradition and common law principles. Segregation and other antiblack Jim Crow laws passed by resurgent white Democrats in the South followed a similar pattern, violating basic tenets of common law. Southern racists twisted the language and ideals of local community into a defense of self-rule only for those with economic and political power. Meanwhile, southern support for expansive federal policies from the New Deal exposed a desire for federal largesse, provided that southerners retained a veto on matters of racial justice in their own states.

Black allegiance to the Republican Party, largely unquestioned from the Civil War through 1932, after that point shifted to the Democratic Party, even as white southerners continued their long rejection of the Republican Party on account of its support for civil rights. But, by the 1960s, the Democratic Party, increasingly influenced by black Americans' growing political voice, began pushing for federal power to end Jim Crow. White southerners who cared about states' rights gravitated toward a Republican Party that had become more focused on federalism and antistatism.

Southern intellectuals, who earlier had become part of the emerging intellectual conservative movement, for all their contributions had failed to defend the longer Anglo-American tradition that understood both slavery and racial separation as deep violations of the natural law. The most eloquent defenders of tradition in the conservative movement were often nevertheless inadequate to the task because they could not see past their history of race relations to a longer pattern of traditional conservatism. Southern conservatism was not inadequate because of its traditionalism, as some assert, but because of its inadequate and narrow traditionalism. Southern conservatives, taken as a whole, failed to reclaim their deepest patrimony.

Increasingly influential over the course of the 1960s and 1970s, southern whites tended not to engage actively with arguments for tradition, instead embracing local and state rights to self-rule, which they blended with religious beliefs that largely defined their politics. The most important example is abortion. In 1973, when the Supreme Court in *Roe v. Wade* struck down the right of any state or locality to make its own laws governing abortion and asserted a national right of access to abortion procedures, many southern evangelicals became political activists for the first time. The Court's decision undermined the democratic process by inventing an absolute, universal right. In doing so, it also made it impossible for Americans to engage politically with this deeply moral issue within their own states or communities. From now on this crucial fight would be national. Responding to this and similar issues (especially local control of public schools), a new bloc of southern voters became less interested in the racial question and more focused on other moral questions.

From a political and cultural perspective, it is sadly irrelevant that southern whites often were motivated by high political principles. Race was never far from the surface, and the conservative movement's ability to formulate consistent principles and put them into action was complicated by a new dependence on southern white electoral support. Conservative arguments were sidelined or never formulated, and, especially where race was concerned, the conservative movement became less conservative than antileftist. Whether principled conservatives might have done more to reclaim and innovate in this era is a question complicated by political and electoral calculations. The fact is that the most sustained conservative arguments largely ignored this problem, leaving it to right-wing liberals to offer the strongest antiracist arguments in the movement. Thus any drive to unravel racist policies and institutions was swallowed up in a wider judicial attack on self-ruling local communities. Academia, the press, and the federal courts now identified self-rule with racism itself.

During the 1970s, strategists in the conservative movement,

frustrated by intrusive Great Society programs begun under the Johnson administration, judicial activism, the ever-expanding administrative state, and increased hostility to the goal of winning the Cold War, began to take action. These political operatives raised massive amounts of new money, with most of it going to antistatist think tanks or political groups. At about the same time, the American economy was struggling with emerging global realities. The structural advantages that had once spurred the expansion of a middle class tied to stable corporations were no longer in play. Production limits imposed by OPEC, the cartel of oil-producing nations, had done away with the cheap energy that had supported the postwar expansion. The costs of a national welfare state, not only in dollars and productivity but in character development, began to show in chronic dependency and reduced productivity. American corporations, bloated and dysfunctional, faced new manufacturing competition from innovative, state-supported companies in Japan and Europe.

Faced with an emergent "age of limits," members of the conservative movement began rethinking the American postwar model of capitalism. Brilliant economists like Milton Friedman sparked interest in free markets, supply-side economics, and sharp reductions of government regulation to spur competitive efficiency. Well-funded think tanks like the Heritage Foundation emerged, propagating both free-market economics and (often neoconservative) scholarly critiques of more radical Great Society social programs while expanding support for the Cold War to include the exporting of democracy to the world. Heritage and other think tanks crafted a coherent set of public policies that assumed American decline was the result of bad government policies and that releasing American industry and the American people from liberal tinkering would bring back American greatness. A policy program was set for the conservative movement through the 1980s and beyond: lower taxes (which would spur investment and spending), reduced regulations (which would lower costs to manufacturing), and winning the Cold War.

These were the proposals that propelled Reagan to the White House and that motivated his administration. The diverse coalition that formulated them, and put them into concrete form for Reagan, only partially overlapped with the conservative movement as originally understood. It included neoconservatives (essentially Cold War liberals) who rejected domestic radicalism while supporting big government at home and expansionism abroad, free-market libertarians, and religious "social issue" voters who might or might not be aware of the traditional roots of their beliefs. Policy was made by professionals in think tanks, academia, and executive agencies.

The movement's agenda was called neoliberalism by leftists who saw in it, whether carried out in the United States or in Margaret Thatcher's Great Britain, a defense of "liberty" that supports only powerful groups with access to capital and markets. Neoliberalism, the left insisted, did not support the working classes or other vulnerable groups and resulted in a widening wealth gap between the few and the many. It was naked and exploitative capitalism, the left charged, covered in a veil of promised liberty and prosperity. This critique was based on crude, neo-Marxist categories and economic assumptions, though it might have had some relevance in a critique of the species of global capitalism that emerged during the 1990s. It is regrettable that the Republican establishment of the 1980s played almost comically to its overdrawn stereotypes.

Rhetorically, Reagan and the "movement" continued to appeal to orthodox Christian activists worried about the decline in public morals. These activists were most interested in abortion but also were active in fighting pornography and cared deeply about who controlled what was taught in public schools. Usually very supportive of Reagan, they saw few tangible results from his administration. Conservatives were part of the mix but largely served as ornaments in the key institutions of movement conservatism. They were called on to define and defend the great principles of Western civilization and to give the movement a semblance of continuity with the sources of a great and ongoing civilization. But the movement was focused on economic and foreign policy goals; attention to moral issues was largely for show.

Reagan's foreign policy was a serious departure from earlier administrations of both parties. Rejecting a policy of containment or peaceful coexistence, Reagan resolutely worked toward defeating the Soviet Union and discrediting communism around the world. Reagan's emphasis on actually winning the Cold War was fully compatible with longstanding conservative principles; the collapse of communism in Eastern Europe, followed quickly by the end of the Soviet Union, justified Reagan's approach, and largely marked the end of an epoch. However, Reagan was a true believer in democracy as a universal good suited to all peoples in all circumstances. This ideological assertion, useful as political rhetoric, was both inconsistent with conservatism and productive of a conspicuously progressive and imperialistic agenda in the 2000s.

In one respect, Reagan was a pitch-perfect defender of conservatism. He contextualized his three-part agenda within a richly American narrative of strong families and vibrant communities – of people taking care of themselves and each other. The major economic and geopolitical successes of the Reagan years vouched for the deeper truth that America's problems were caused not by failures of the people but by those of their leaders. Reagan may not have understood the great conservative tradition well, but he felt American norms of self-rule in his bones. When he spoke of American identity or his own life journey he became a master mythmaker who told a story a great majority of Americans could recognize as their own.

Had Buckley's vision of an intellectual and political movement that expressed the deeper conservatism of the American people come to pass? Or has Reagan's dramatic political success distorted our view of the recent past? A few words on the costs of Reagan's success are necessary before we explore the movement and conservatism after his presidency.

In 1955, when Buckley lamented that America's intellectual and political elites were out of step with the people's conservatism, he launched *National Review* as an intellectual and political challenge to those elites. Conservatives and others who would become part of the conservative movement produced an intellectual rebirth that spawned key institutions like ISI (originally the Intercollegiate Society of Individualists and now the Intercollegiate Studies Institute), which aimed to educate college students about Western civilization and how to sustain its accomplishments.

Dedicated as much to great literature and the imaginative arts as to advocacy for free markets and limited government, ISI represented conservative principles that root political life in deeper human connections. ISI worked to cultivate persons who take responsibility for their lives and who govern themselves well by rooting them in the rich civilizational soil that is their rightful inheritance. ISI is only one example of the institutional and intellectual flourishing of diverse groups on the right, from conservative to libertarian, from humane to economic, that suggested the vitality of the movement in the 1950s and 1960s.

No such richness can be found in the 1980s or since, though

most of the institutions founded in those early years still exist. The focus of the movement turned overwhelmingly to political matters, narrowing and coarsening conservatism. The big money went to influential policy centers like Heritage and the American Enterprise Institute (AEI). Most talented young people on the right went into politics and policy, almost always without substantive education in conservative traditions. Even the grand political success of the Reagan presidency (and we should not underestimate the degree to which the movement altered American political life) was strictly limited in scope. The resultant political regime did not address social issues seriously, nor did the movement meaningfully address the takeover of key institutions by the American left, which would turn out to be catastrophic for the movement and for the nation as a whole.

To achieve political success, the movement increasingly replaced complex ideas with simple slogans, focused attention on a few big political goals (taxes, deregulation, and winning the Cold War), and lost sight of the array of political and social issues crucial to the healthy functioning of American society. Even as the movement rose to power, indices of social pathology continued to rise, from divorce and illegitimacy rates to maldistribution of wealth, to say nothing of a string of court losses that undermined important conservative principles. The success of the movement was not necessarily the success of those principles.

Conservatives should have recognized both the opportunities and the limits of political success. There should have been a reassessment aimed at taking advantage of new opportunities to move closer to the American people, to govern with conservative principles. Unfortunately, this didn't happen. Failure on this front was an important cause of the failures of succeeding Republican administrations and, indeed, of events leading to the political earthquake of the 2016 presidential election.

As we argue in the next chapter, the series of failed administrations following Reagan – both Republican and Democrat – sought to sideline or bury conservative principles and their spokesmen. But the principles, and the traditions in which they are rooted, continue to exist, even if they are embattled. Reactions to these failures have uncovered a past we had overlooked because the new establishment had come to believe that its ideology was the natural political center rather than a powerful response to specific conditions. In this revised understanding of history – call it a new past – we find deeper currents at work, deeper conservative traditions and continuities. We can reclaim this past and with it the lost soul of our tradition.

CHAPTER SEVEN

After the Cold War
Right-Wing Liberalism and Its Failures

C old War conservatism gained the world and lost its soul. Successful in electoral politics, victorious in the Cold War, and highly profitable for many of its members, the conservative movement was an alliance that suppressed dissent and inconvenient principles in the name of unity and situational relevance. The problems it faced were very real. The threat of nuclear war with a weaponized ideology dedicated to the destruction of our way of life; rising support for a permanent, centralized welfare and administrative state; political and cultural splintering along racial, ethnic, and gender lines – all called for extraordinary measures and the temporary suspension of some deeply held principles.

The conservative movement increasingly became the ideological arm of the Republican Party. Ever at odds with more liberal, establishment Republicans, the conservative movement's leaders nevertheless tied themselves to the party, further suppressing dissent in their ranks as they pursued political relevance of the most superficial kind. Concentrating money and energy in the cause of political influence brought real success at the polls and in the fight against communism, but only modest achievements in the struggle to bring constitutional limits to the federal government. Unfortunately, the political success (if not policy accomplishments) of the Republican Party agenda reinforced the tendency in politics toward slogans and abstractions. Republicans mistook a situational conservatism with conservatism itself. Blinded also by their own vested interests in emerging global markets, Republicans largely jettisoned the historically textured principles of conservatism for the liberating abstractions of right-wing liberalism. Republican ideology was simple, marketable, and, for many, profitable. Throwing over the cultural and intellectual ballast of traditionalists and other conservatives allowed Republicans to rise quickly to short-term electoral success. It also denied Republican leaders the grounding they needed to face changing circumstances, or to challenge their own ahistorical assumptions.

Republican Party ideology rested on a simplistic version of the conservative liberty narrative. Rather than conceive of liberties as historical products to be passed down, along with the culture and character that give them meaning, Republican Party ideology is emancipatory; it conceives of the past as something to overcome. In this way, the progressive and the Republican ideologies mirror one another, with each promising liberation, one from inequality and the other from limits on individual freedom.

To liberate the individual is, for both these ideologies, the highest expression of the American idea. Projected internationally, America takes on a unique global role to liberate all unfree people from repressive regimes. Policies supporting the conservative movement's vision of America, such as lower taxes and fewer regulations, were situated within a most *unconservative* vision: that "we have the power to make the world anew" (a quotation from Reagan channeling the radical Thomas Paine). Unleashing the individual to pursue its life and interests would

likewise unleash unimagined productivity, technological transformation, greater wealth, and greater comfort.

This ideology was simple, seemingly rooted in human
nature itself – or at least individuals' natural aspirations to self-
mastery and self-assertion. But it lacked any compelling
description of what makes liberty achievable and worth pursuing as a high political accomplishment. Institutions, norms,
civilization itself, all became mere background to the story of
national, then individual liberation. Sharing with the conservative tradition the high principle of self-rule and ordered liberty,
Republican Party ideology deemphasized the inherited, civilizational order necessary for liberty to be a virtue.

The Soviet Union's collapse in 1991 made the past seem
unimportant; victory in this grand ideological conflict was
taken as a sign that liberty was natural and universal, not particular and historical. Believing that one knows the natural and
universal human good and that the United States is the shining
"city on a hill" encourages pride in nation without the angst of
its checkered past. If America is an idea, then it is not bound to
its past failures. The injustices of the past are not our failures,
only previous generations' lack of fidelity to the natural principles expressed in the idea of America. For those who believe
in the idea, it is always, as the Reagan campaign advertisement
put it, "morning in America."

Of all those who belonged to the movement, none focused
more on the American idea (and "American exceptionalism")
than a new generation of so-called neoconservatives. Like the
first generation, they were mainly academics, but unlike their
forebears they were almost exclusively focused on foreign policy. A small group, confined to think tanks and academic posts,
the neoconservatives were critics of the foreign policies of both

George H. W. Bush and Bill Clinton. Having developed a view of international relations stressing the necessary American role as the hegemonic power after the Cold War, neoconservatives placed the American idea at the center of global policy. They sought to use American power to police the world and, just as important, to push the concept of a redeemer nation spreading democracy. Democracies, so their theory went, do not go to war with other democracies and tend to make better trading partners. Thus, they argued, both self-interest and virtue – indeed, destiny – dictated that Americans spread their idea throughout the world.

Freed from any clear security threat to the United States, most Republican leaders turned their attention toward globalism, trade, and constructing through treaties and other mechanisms a new world order – a world made safe for global capitalism. Neoconservatives were left with a geopolitical theory but no means of justifying their more imperial conceptions of America's role in the world. For more than a decade the neoconservatives wandered in the political desert.

Meanwhile, a conservative alternative to Republican orthodoxy also emerged. A new global reality offered a return path to longstanding American conservative traditions. In practice this would mean a strong but smaller military, a foreign policy that does not seek to alter the internal affairs of other regimes, and a reduction in government surveillance obligations and capabilities. America is not, in this view, a redeemer nation, and its system of government and liberties are the result of a long history and not the natural condition of all humans. For the conservative, to fight for a universal human freedom risks wreaking havoc abroad and losing American liberties at home. American liberties can persist only if Americans understand, support, and cultivate our unique tradition and the social and cultural underpinnings of this rare species of self-rule. Simplistic abstractions are neither suited to the human condition nor capable of forming a sturdy foundation for liberty.

Following the terrorist attacks on the United States on September 11, 2001, the relative influence of these competing perspectives changed quickly and dramatically. The conservative argument not only lost its small influence in the movement but became the object of derision – it was cast out of the conversation. Meanwhile, neoconservatives had developed a very coherent foreign policy during their years in the wilderness. They were well placed to answer all the new questions suddenly faced by the George W. Bush administration. More influential than their numbers would suggest, neoconservatives fought with the establishment realists within the Republican Party, making this its great divide until the political earthquake of 2016. Accepting the principle of preemptive war (long advocated by neoconservatives), President Bush suddenly reversed course on the issue of regime change, embracing it as a primary objective of foreign policy. Clearly, neoconservative ideas had won the day in his administration.

Economic changes in the 1970s and 1980s had already suggested the possibility of a second age of globalism, and by the early 1990s the world was again experiencing the benefits and challenges of economic globalization. Capital flows were increasingly international, as was the market for labor. Corporations found it increasingly easy and profitable to move manufacturing to poor countries offering very cheap labor with few environmental and safety regulations. As with the first age of globalism, transportation costs dropped, and multilateral agreements created vast trade zones that almost eliminated barriers to doing business across national boundaries. As corporate ownership and manufacturing became more global, corporations' national identities became more fluid. Further contributing to this fluid identity, corporations shopped countries for the best tax structures and often located their headquarters in countries where they had little or no business interests.

Just as the first globalist age produced dramatic increases in wealth, productivity, innovation, and technological progress, so also did this one. Both ages also produced greater separation between the wealthiest and poorest peoples and undermined the ability of working people to maintain their standard of living and ways of life. The result was a new class system – one based as much in cultural background and assumptions as in economic function.

The greatest flows of wealth from second-wave globalization went to capitalists whose economic interests and personal predilections were neither local nor national. This was in marked contrast to first-wave globalization. Moreover, the model of the new megarich capitalist was different. Overwhelmingly products of university education and concentrated in industries that require constant technological innovation to survive, second-wave capitalists are prone to focus on the transformative power of human knowledge and technology. The past, even the recent past, is dead to them. The speed of innovation means that almost nothing inherited is of value – neither machines nor organizational methods nor assumptions about the long-term viability of a given company or product. Obsessive focus on the future, and on their own transformative power, has shaped this small elite to see in itself a new model for human development – even producing dreams of becoming transhuman.

In the fields of high tech, finance, a variety of manufacturing and service industries, journalism, education, and government service, there has been an intoxication with power and transformation, a new outlook according to which neither history nor nature are normative. Elites in these institutions have rejected both liberalism and conservatism in favor of a progressive modernism that views the highest human purpose as the power to create an imagined future.

It is significant that these institutions were the very ones that leftists took over during the decades when the conservative movement began its journey toward political relevance. The most obvious institutional takeover was in higher education. Through much of the twentieth century, the intellectual center of American colleges and universities had been liberal, with a broad acceptance of conservatives and various leftists. Conservatives had influence in most departments, at least in non-elite schools, for the first half of the century, and well into the 1970s conservatives were important parts of the faculty at most universities.

The conquest by the left began in earnest in the late 1960s, and by the end of the Reagan era one was hard pressed to find many conservatives in elite universities, even (and perhaps especially) in fields where conservatives had long been deeply influential, like literature and the humanities in general. Since the late 1980s and 1990s, liberals have lost their own central role in higher education, leaving leftists determined and equipped to use naked power to transform society in all its aspects in the name of social justice. From these incubators of leftism have come our newest generation of global capitalists: rich and deracinated, powerful but unwise, well-trained but without the civilizing power of classical education, moralistic without character.

The leftist capture of the legal profession, while not so complete, has created a power utterly hostile to inherited conservative principles. Today judges operate without compelling constitutional or democratic barriers to their usurping of legislative power. Even more basic has been the interest of leftists in controlling public schools. Leftists have worked to transform our provincial, custom-bound, and supposedly irrational population into one more to their liking. In the process they have built an educational system designed to overcome the influence of family, religion, and tradition. As movement (or Republican) conservatism took power politically, the influential institutions that shape our social and cultural order were lost to the left, often without a fight.

More visible today is the ideological narrowness of the media. For decades news organizations served as guardians of public messaging and the clearinghouse for what they considered proper news. A new generation of journalists, trained in leftist universities and confronting an emerging alternative media, behave today – particularly since the beginning of the 2016 election cycle – as ideologues who are in a struggle for power. As in the university, love of power has defeated love of truth.

Leftists have formed an interlocking network of institutions dedicated to transforming America. They have real power, which they have exercised for a couple of generations now, to weaken the social fabric and institutional supports that make possible a self-governing people. Judicial activism has done a great deal, since the 1970s, to undermine both self-governing communities and the functionality and sustainability of families. The expansion of the regulatory state, which movement conservatism slowed but did not stop, provided an opening for those who see in the power to regulate the means to circumvent norms and the people's wishes and foist on them a new moral code that fits the left's own notion of social justice.

As the federal and state governments have usurped a host of social functions, they have crowded out the voluntary and private associations in which people learn neighborliness as they solve their problems together. Instead of associations that connect people with one another to solve problems in common, leftist ideology, now deeply infecting American governments, encourages solidarity based on identity politics – a solidarity that in fact separates people by categories of race, sexual preference, or any number of other markers. We face a politically correct environment that excludes meaningful pluralism in favor of a perverse concentration on grievances for which no answer is offered, except ever more power and money, and above all the pleasure of hating well.

Traditional Americans who want to be self-reliant, who want economic opportunities that allow them to take care of their families and needs, who want to be part of a thick community of reciprocity, who believe in God and gain strength and comfort from their religious community, and who want to trust others and accept that a person's word is that person's bond – these Americans have been told that they are perverse and in need of reeducation. Traditional Americans confront elites in all sorts of institutions who treat them, their beliefs, their religion, and in some cases their very skin, as malicious. They are told to hate their own heritage, to abandon centuries-old moral beliefs, and to get out of the way of progress. They are told to accept cultural extinction.

Traditional Americans certainly are not limited to the much-caricatured white male. In fact traditional women have a particularly rough path in our society. They are pressured from a young age to cast aside long-held norms and morals, to reject the idea that they might want to seek men who can provide for them. Should they marry a man with the financial means to serve as the sole breadwinner (something increasingly uncommon), they are told they lack strength, initiative, or intelligence. Whereas once womanhood was associated with a life focused on child-rearing and active participation in the life of church and local community, to choose such a life is now seen as a betrayal of womanhood. As for members of minority groups, black and Hispanic Americans especially are told that resentment must characterize their attitude toward the larger society, that they must reject the American way of life that is their birthright as much as any other citizen's. Too many are trapped in lives of government dependency; those who succeed through hard work often must contend with suspicions that their achievements are not really their own but rather the product of affirmative action policies instituted by the government.

The American public philosophy, that every American should have the opportunity for success through hard work within community, has been torn apart. The tradition bequeathed to us, of self-government rooted in virtue and aimed at personal improvement through pursuit of the common good, has been disparaged to the point where it is the butt of jokes. Even as they fail in their fundamental tasks of upholding the law, protecting people's physical security, and spending within the government's own means, partisans and government functionaries seek further, ever more insulated power over our daily lives; they wish to take from us the last vestiges of self-government.

Victory in the Cold War was no small thing. Unfortunately, while the conservative movement was moving toward the center of power and simplifying ideas in pursuit of that victory, it failed to work for domestic reform – a neglect that cost the movement its soul. We can and must reclaim that soul by enlivening our tradition and facing down the forces of centralization and alienation that confront us. To do so we must glean lessons from America's past, especially as seen through the lens of conservatism's development and deformation over recent decades. In this way we may formulate policies and reformulate principles that can serve us in the struggle ahead.

CHAPTER EIGHT

Gleaning Virtues
What Conservatism Is, and Is About

The conservative movement failed because its leaders forgot that political power itself is not an end. Political power, like all power, is good only when and to the extent it is used in pursuit of its proper goal. Victory in the Cold War surely was an important accomplishment, in keeping with the government's duty to protect its people from annihilation. But national defense is only part of the proper goal of political power. And beyond this signal victory, the conservative movement has little to show for its years in power.

Philosophers, saints, and regular people have long known that political power's proper goal is service to the common good. What, then, is the common good? When they abandoned conservative principles, movement leaders set aside the American tradition of self-governing communities, in which persons in their families, churches, and local associations pursued a variety of common ends, making up a flourishing, common life. In effect, they set aside pursuit of the common good as it has been understood for centuries in American society and even longer in Western civilization. In its place, these right-wing liberals set a vision of autonomous individuals pursuing material well-being, safe within the confines of a protective administrative and welfare state. This is a vision of alienation, in which each of us is abandoned to our own devices, left alone to face a world bereft of meaningful communities. It is a kind of home-lessness – and it has driven all too many Americans to the ersatz community of progressivism, in which the state tends to our needs and wants, taking from us that central element of the good life for Americans, self-government.

Rebuilding our home begins with the realization that politics is not about making the good life for the people; it is about protecting the natural associations within which a self-govern-ing people can pursue a good life on its own. Our Constitu-tion's great wisdom lies in its structure – in its federalism and its enumeration of specific, limited goals and powers the cen-tral government may pursue, leaving the rest to the states and, especially, townships. That structure is suited only to a self-governing people, grounded in religious tradition, a sense of place, and a sense of its own history.

Today, a usable conservatism must begin by reclaiming our heritage and by developing the richness of our story in a way that exposes the dangerous half-truths of political abstractions. Conservatives believe in natural rights, in freedom, and in our equality before God. We also recognize the limitations of these principles. All of us are fallen creatures, different and unequal in countless ways that shape outcomes. Any decent society must take into account these facts of our nature.

Conservatives recognize a truth that is perhaps most diffi-cult to grasp in these times of alienation: humans are historical beings who need to know their story to live well. We know that our civilization, however imperfect, supplies the necessary conditions for our current culture and is an unimaginably pre-cious gift that we receive along with the duty to preserve it and to pass it on to our children. Americans can have no meaning-ful conservatism without this understanding of our tradition's contextual richness, this account of human life that places the natural or the universal within the framework of living traditions that give particular and usable shape to the truths of our collective lives.

To rebuild our home, conservatives must concentrate on institutions and associations that, first, cultivate the art of self-governance in community and, second, mold the social and cultural forces that are upstream from politics and policy. To enliven these associations will require a fight against governments that try to change their nature and also that we push government out of areas of our lives where other institutions can thrive. As Buckley understood, much of conservatism consists in the willingness to say no to policies that seem to be aimed at promoting good things. As we argue in Part II of this book, however, it is not a question of whether we ought to do good things, but of which good things we ought to pursue, and how.

In abandoning conservative principles for a seemingly more palatable right-wing liberalism, the conservative movement perpetuated the mistaken notion that opposition to "big government" is by nature heartless. Conservatives are not "against" protecting the weak and the poor. We are not "against" educating our children or tending to the sick. Conservatives are "for" communities that take seriously the duty of all their members to undertake every one of these important tasks. And we recognize that a distant national government that attempts to achieve these ends will do so through impersonal bureaucratic mechanisms that dehumanize everyone involved even as they undermine the ability of self-governing communities to form and shape the characters of their members. Reclaiming our soul entails rethinking not just what is good to do but how we should go about doing it.

The good life is pursued in local communities. This does not mean, however, that there is no role for the nation. Indeed, it is crucial that we Americans rethink what it means to be an American. Conservatives must become the storytellers of our national identity. We must reclaim our own history of conservative principles emerging out of the experiences and norms of a living tradition, but we also must concentrate on reaching larger publics with better stories of our national heritage, better ways of understanding our past and the purchase of that past on our present and our future. We must tell truthful stories that ascend to truthful myths about who we are. The pious Pilgrim, the frontiersman and -woman, the entrepreneur, the immigrant worker seeking to become fully American, all are parts of our story. They help make up a larger story of a nation in which communities are free to pursue their own visions, in which the restless may find a road to travel as the tired may find a place to rest. The story is one of a tradition, a set of customs, norms, and beliefs in which broad social equality is the basis for meaningful difference, in which individual effort combines with a spirit of volunteerism for one's community, in which progress means a drive for improvement tied to the permanent things laid down in faith, family, and freedom as expressed through self-government.

Conservatives cannot lead our nation until they provide a compelling account of our national identity. Only after we know who we are can we look meaningfully to a future that we help craft in this age of conservative revolution. In crisis we reclaim. In reclaiming we innovate. In innovating we preserve and hand down.

PART II

REBUILDING OUR CULTURAL HOME

The Return to Human Nature

CHAPTER NINE

Reclaiming the Township

The most perceptive analysis of America's democratic culture came from a young Frenchman, Alexis de Tocqueville, in the 1830s. His two-volume *Democracy in America* remains the most important work concerning the character and fate of democracy in the modern world, but it was his particularly keen insight into the relationship between American mores and American institutions that warrants our attention today. Tocqueville found in America a great many puzzles and a species of democracy and equality utterly alien to Europeans. Americans, for instance, combine and harmonize the "spirit of religion" with the "spirit of freedom," two forces constantly at odds elsewhere in the world. But most hopeful of all, Americans had done the impossible: Americans loved both equality and freedom, holding them in a salutary tension that no other culture has ever sustained so well. But how?

Nothing about America struck Tocqueville more powerfully than its vital, self-governing townships. Small, generally nonurban communities enjoying some powers of self-rule, townships were the foundation of self-government in America. Tocqueville recognized them as the most natural and universal of primary associations; wherever you find any substantial number of people in a given locality, they will have formed a township, with its own rules and customs, so that they can tend to their common needs. But in America the township took an especially powerful form. Where most townships quickly fall under the control of a central government, those in America were sufficiently isolated and independent to maintain meaningful self-rule. American townships retained responsibility for their own public welfare in everything from road-building to religious observance to educating children and caring for the poor. Recognizing the necessity of sharing the burdens of local life, Americans developed the habits, character, and tastes necessary to participate fully in the variety of associations making up the township and, through it, the community of communities that was the American republic.

Crucially, Americans' love of "township freedom" – the term Tocqueville used to refer to the freedom of the community to rule itself – was prior to, and higher than, their love of individual freedom. No distinction is more important than this one for today's struggle to maintain three centuries of self-rule. As Tocqueville observed on his travels about the country, citizens of each town developed the taste and habit of participating deeply in a self-governing community, and each citizen developed a special pride in this collective empowerment.

Tocqueville likened this attachment to that of people who live in the mountains. The distinctive landscape and features of where they live make it special to them: "ownership" of their mountain is crucial to their affection. Similarly, as each town made its own laws, decided among its members how to divide up administrative duties, and otherwise determined (in relative isolation from other powers) how to form the community, that specific town took on a political shape that made it different from all other towns. To cherish your political freedom prior to and more deeply than your freedom to do what you want without encumbrances is the defining attitude of a self-ruling people. This love of political freedom leads to pride of place, attachment to and affection for your neighbors, and, finally, pride of ownership in your laws because they are the means by which you govern yourself.

Tocqueville noted that American habits, tastes, and affections – their mores – were fostered in institutions and conditions. Had these townships lost power early to a larger government, the taste for, and the habituation to, self-rule would never have developed and America would have largely followed the easy flow of democratic societies toward an administrative state.

Americans always have been wanderers in the sense that we tend to move in pursuit of greener pastures, better jobs, and the like. But for hundreds of years Americans brought with them to new townships the habits of association necessary to make them "work" in the sense of providing a network of relationships, rules, and customs within a specific area and within which more intimate associations of family, church, workplace, and a whole host of spontaneous associations could flourish. Living within such townships, Americans saw one another as members of a series of overlapping associations that made up one community. In an important sense they saw other members of their township as friends with whom they shared a common life, rather than strangers with whom they might share a specific interest or goal. The township was not just a place, it was home.

Today many Americans see themselves as "citizens of the world," as if we could form meaningful relationships with billions of people of whose values and ways of life we know nothing beyond what we are told by travelogues and by ideologues in the classroom. Sold on visions of individual autonomy, superficial multiculturalism, online "communities," and an ethic of "social justice" suspicious of local eccentricities, too many Americans dismiss township life as socially narrow and boring, or insufficiently "diverse," and look to the national government to guarantee that "the locals" abide by uniform rules laid down by some centralized bureaucracy. But, whatever digital visionaries may dream of, we must all live and work in a specific place where we own or use property and interact with the physical world around us. To the extent we look to some distant government to tend to our character and needs, we lose the habits of face-to-face involvement, cooperation, and conflict in which we learn to respect ourselves and other people. We lose the essential, concrete communities in which we become something more than individuals: real persons participating in associations where we belong and have purpose.

The globalist economy works to separate us from local institutions and fellow townspeople. But even in the most homogenized regions of America, with the familiar sights of franchise-filled strip malls and drive-through ATMs and chain big-box stores, we retain important remnants of our townships; indeed, those of us who live outside major urban areas may still live in functioning townships. Here one meets the same people in more than one venue – both at school and in the store, at church and at the coffee shop. Here we must not simply check with the local zoning board about building that new tool shed but ask our neighbor whether it will cause problems if we place it in a specific spot. Here we must live with the people around us, interacting with them in real time and about real, concrete issues. Here, if our township still lives, we experience the intertwining of various associations, functions, and affections.

Those townships that survive are not, however, in good health. State and federal regulations now dictate not only the duties of the local government but the shape of private relations – who may hire whom, how one conducts one's business, and with whom one associates and how. Political centralization began when Americans sought economic security from the national government. It accelerated when largely just demands for legal equality were combined with the desire for guaranteed comfort to extend federal authority over all aspects of local life.

The federal government has claimed the right to regulate the most intimate aspects of our lives in the name of justice and the public welfare. We already have discussed the unjust and unconservative nature of the Jim Crow laws so often invoked as justification for this commanding presence. We note in passing the refusal of the federal government to insist on the rights of freed slaves to the real protections provided by the Constitution under the post–Civil War Fourteenth Amendment, most especially access to courts on equal procedural footing so that they could defend their lives, liberty, and property. The extension of federal power over health, education, and other aspects of the people's welfare was the product of short-term need and a long-term determination to make America conform to an abstract and inhumane blueprint of economic, social, and political equality that undermines the real equality of common membership in community. As for the "rights revolution," it has devolved from rejection of segregation to federal interference on behalf of even the most angry, disruptive individual seeking to force his community to conform to his lifestyle and do nothing that might offend him.

We are no longer talking about living up to our deepest principles of justice, as with the civil rights movement to end Jim Crow. Today we confront a national power that forces on us a transformation rather than a realization: an entirely new society based on principles alien to our culture and our nature, rather than an improved society that keeps our inheritance and principles intact for all Americans.

Progressives work to delegitimize local governments and, more important, to have the national government absorb their power, authority, and reason to exist. Taking over, in the name of fairness and efficiency, the tasks properly belonging to neighbors, bureaucrats in charge of political machinery have degraded townships from the essential means by which we govern ourselves to mere corrupt tools of a higher, national power. Progressives would have us give up our political freedom, our township freedom, to become liberated individuals, disconnected from authority and bound only to the state.

We would not want to add our voices to those who turn the small town into a kind of utopian ideal. Today's townships too often practice needless, hectoring regulation, cronyism, and corruption. But we submit that Podunk Anytown has nothing on New York City or San Francisco when it comes to any of the vices of local governance, and that a substantial part of the problem is not too much local power but too little.

If corruption is rampant in local government, it is because the stakes are so low. Efficiency and morale have sunk because our centralized government has taken over their essential functions. The result is a nation increasingly ruled from afar by an intrusive national government, aided by local functionaries with little real power but all too many privileges and defenses against the people they claim to represent. Citizens robbed of meaningful participation in their own governance, meanwhile, find little to interest them in their own towns.

Robert Nisbet, one of the great sociologists of the twentieth century, pointed out that a community needs, more than anything else, a reason to exist. Having allowed our national government to take over responsibility for educating our children, tending the poor, and seeing to it that none of us acts unjustly toward another, we have empowered a vast, centralized apparatus to take over the roles once played by more natural, local associations. In the process we have lost the habit of associating with our fellows to address our common needs. It was this association that encouraged individuals to become men and women of character with the moral sense necessary for self-government as persons and communities.

Restoring township government must begin with tearing down much of the national edifice built over the second half of the twentieth century. The federal government is simply too much a part of our lives to leave room for our natural and primary associations. So long as Washington is in charge of welfare spending, centralized accrediting agencies dictate what public education will consist of, the US Supreme Court dictates what prayers can be said where, and a host of agencies determine when a person's choice not to participate in a given relationship constitutes "discrimination," local government and voluntary associations will have little reason to exist. They will be left to find what reward they can in administering federal policies and gaining whatever power and wealth they can for themselves. When the public is robbed of its function in a local community it ceases to be a public. It is no longer capable of turning strangers into neighbors.

Local social services boards, school boards, zoning boards, and all the humble cogs in the machinery of local administration perform so badly because they are asked to perform so little, because they are mere cogs in national machinery. Only if these associations are freed from federal control and returned to their proper place and role as creatures of their own local constituents can they address local affairs in cooperation with the people. Only then can we regain the concrete practices of self-government and the character it builds. Only then can we truly come home.

CHAPTER TEN

The Forgotten Natural Family

Why do we marry? Why should we value families? Americans seem to have become unclear on the answers to these fundamental questions. We debate whether the government should tolerate people who refuse to help celebrate same-sex unions and we argue over how to address violence, depression, and dependency on government assistance, especially among young people raised without fathers. But we shy away from asking whether we have made life better or worse for young people – and ourselves – by viewing the family through the lenses of public recognition and public policy rather than our understanding of who we are and what makes life worth living.

Conflict over the family stems from the persistence of two fundamentally conflicting visions of its nature and purpose. Law and popular culture currently favor a view of the family as a loosely defined social grouping, often but not always biological, that provides mutual support and primary care for children. Marriage, on this reading, is a public affirmation of the commitment of two people to one another, which commitment may or may not be long-lasting, but which both parties at the time wish to have solemnized and celebrated. The other, older vision of the family is both more organic and more spiritual. It sees marriage and family as intrinsically tied together and rooted in the natural drive to procreate and raise one's children

in common to carry on the family, the society, and the civilization of which one is a part. This latter vision, of the family as
both natural association and primary institution – as the community we naturally form and the fundamental unit of society –
is held in increasing disfavor. It has been obscured by decades
of misguided public policy and by an ideology of atomistic
individualism. Regaining clarity and reclaiming the traditional
understanding of the family are essential to reestablishing the
basic norms necessary for a peaceful, self-governing people.

It is simplest to begin with the vision of the family popular
in the 2010s. Supreme Court Justice Anthony Kennedy summed
it up in the 2015 decision *Obergefell v. Hodges*, which decreed
that all states must issue marriage licenses to same-sex couples.
Writing for the majority, Justice Kennedy stated that marriage
is a means by which individuals "define and express their identity." Other "ideals" also may be embodied in the legally constituted family, but, Kennedy held, the "fundamental right" to
marry is rooted in individuals' natural drive for self-expression.

For decades, the Supreme Court has been handing down
decisions similarly focused on the individual. In *Planned Parenthood of Southeastern Pennsylvania v. Casey*, in 1992, the Court
ruled that "[a]t the heart of liberty is the right to define one's
own concept of existence, of meaning, of the universe, and of
the mystery of human life." America, on this view, is dedicated
to the proposition that the fundamental unit of society – the
proper object of rights, of protection, and of concern – is the
individual. That individual achieves fulfillment in defining and
expressing itself. As to the individual's social drives, they are
aimed at the individual's own flourishing through forming,
shaping, and ending a variety of relationships designed to
enrich the lives of those involved in them.

The contemporary family is one, but only one, of these relationships. It is an ever-shifting, dissolving, and potentially re-forming opportunity for self-expression. It may give rise to deep feelings and even a sense of duty but itself is subordinate to the adult members' individual needs, which are understood as the defining moral needs. Society, being dedicated to the flourishing of the individual, must support and approve that individual's choices. And so, as several cases that gained national attention in the 2010s attest, to many it seems natural to punish florists, photographers, and bakers who cannot in good conscience participate in celebrating same-sex unions, as those who invoked their conscience felt they were being asked to do. It seems only fair to do away with "patriarchal" father-daughter dances. And it seems a matter of justice to take children away from would-be adoptive parents who refuse to provide access to sex-altering treatments. As this kind of thinking goes, the government has a special obligation to protect individuals from beliefs and commitments that limit their full creative expression of identity. To be genuinely free, the government must force us to be free.

Why, then, do some Americans, potentially at the cost of their jobs, reputations, and businesses, refuse to celebrate this contemporary family? The mainstream answer is that they are either hateful bigots or (to many people the same thing) religious zealots. The real reason has to do with that older, generally but not exclusively religion-based, vision of the family.

Since long before America was founded, families in our civilization – in all civilizations – have consisted of mothers, fathers, and their offspring, generally supplemented and reinforced by grandparents and other blood relations. Though cultures give to families variations on conventional forms by circumstance and need, the institution is natural, responding to human needs and helping to fulfill human wants. Through families, men and women become part of a greater whole, as suited to our nature as both social and cultural animals. Through this primary institution children learn who they are and how to be virtuous members of their society. When the sex drive is restrained, or rather directed by its natural consequence – children to be loved, cherished, and nurtured – social bonds develop, community flourishes, and a society of decent, caring people becomes possible: the ever visible dream discovered in the highest aspirations born of our nature.

This family is not some abstract ideal. Family members inevitably disagree with one another and, as with any human institution, there is no such thing as perfection: tragedy can alter families, and in some families people will commit or suffer from abuse. But neither is the family simply a collection of individuals sharing certain needs, beliefs, and experiences as they pursue their own flourishing. Any functioning family is greater than the sum of its parts. Husbands sacrifice for their wives, wives for their husbands, and both for their children out of love, but also out of duty and habit more than grandiose ideological or emotional leaps. The natural family does not merely fulfill our need for self-expression. It makes us more fully human by taking us out of ourselves and into something larger and more constitutive of character and virtue than our desires for recognition and emotional support.

Natural as it is, then, the family is demanding. It also is essential to the formation and maintenance of a self-governing, virtuous society. By rearing children to be virtuous adults, the natural family makes possible a civil social order. Both parents must take part, over time, in the raising of children. And they cannot do this fully unless they are fully committed to playing a developing but consistent role in this lifelong community.

It is the example of a strong, responsible father who instills the habits of hard work and responsibility that leads young men to become protectors rather than abusers. It is the example of a strong, responsible mother who instills the habits of caring and restraint that leads young women to become nurturers rather than users or the abused. It is the example and experience of a strong family in which each does his or her part to serve the common good that teaches all young people to place the interests of others (especially their children) above their own.

No people can govern itself – can maintain a decent, civil order – if its members have not learned to govern themselves as persons, which means as members of families. If the vast majority of the people fail to obey the law the vast majority of the time, chaos will reign; in such a scenario, no society could long afford enough police to prevent and contain crime. To the extent people come to see restraint on their personal inclinations as evil, government will resort to spying and other intrusive methods (e.g., video surveillance on the street, in shops, and on personal devices) to keep the people under watch. America's recent experience with FBI and other secret surveillance shows that democracies are not immune to the creep of political oversight. The alternative to authoritarianism is trust rooted in virtue. Only if we can trust most everyone to obey the law even when no one is looking can the law serve its purpose. And only when we can trust most everyone to behave decently even if there is no effective law (say, requiring a man to support his children) can we have a decent society.

But if the natural family is so natural, and if its benefits are so essential, then how did so many Americans come to see it as spiritually stultifying and even oppressive? How is it that today it so often fails, or fails to form, or is rejected altogether? Families always have had problems, and people always have had problems with their families. This is natural in a fallen world.

The difference today is that so many people have rejected or rather forgotten what a family is supposed to be because they have lost contact with human nature.

It is possible to lose sight of an association's nature and importance if we focus only on our own short-term interests and rights. For decades now, we have enforced policies that undermine the family and propagated an ideology that portrays it as unnatural and even sinister. It began with the best intentions, of supporting widows and abandoned mothers. Over time, however, policy mistakes, rooted in the idea that the federal government can fill in for dissolving families, have taken their toll. Welfare benefits intended to help single mothers have kept fathers away from their children. No-fault divorce laws intended to free members of already broken families have encouraged both spouses to treat marriage as a mere contract either party can break without penalty. And a sexual revolution has undermined cooperation in child rearing and the very idea of sex as a biological category.

Too many Americans refrain from defending or even defining the natural family for fear of being labeled sexist or homophobic. But there is nothing in the understanding of natural sex roles that denies the equality of all persons in the sight of God. Nothing, here, dictates or even excuses intolerance toward others. The basis of proper tolerance is an understanding of the limited but real natural differences between men and women; that understanding is necessary if we are to raise children capable of respecting one another and themselves.

One need not disapprove of, let alone suppress, other relationships merely because one recognizes that they are not familial. Many important relationships, be they social, religious, or political, are not familial. And families themselves may encounter tragedy through the death or abandonment of a spouse, the inability to have children, or other causes. Relatives, friends, and the community may have to step in to provide succor and support in such circumstances. We can acknowledge such circumstances while still holding that something crucial is lost if we strip from the family our understanding of its essential, natural purpose. That loss affects more than family members themselves. Even as it leaves children without appropriate role models, it also leaves society without properly formed young people. Because families are not only a natural but, for self-governing people, a primary institution in the cultivation of requisite civic virtues, the undermining of this institution must necessarily lead to the collapse of a free and self-governing society.

It is wrong to see the family as merely the source of social goods like education, emotional stability, and training for responsible adulthood. That kind of utilitarian calculus runs up against the claim that states, communities, or other organizations can "do the job" of raising kids without family ties. Sometimes, in limited numbers and with great dedication, communities (though rarely large bureaucratic systems) can help already strong children thrive. Moreover, the family that is valued solely or even principally for its side benefits will not last long in the face of the promptings and temptations of our individualistic, sex-drenched culture.

And yet it remains a primary fact of our human nature that no society can flourish unless the vast majority of its children are raised as parts of permanent, natural families. A society like ours, in which children are so often raised without one steady, committed father, will suffer from massive cultural dislocation. All too many young people will fail to form families of their own. Too many young men will turn to violence as young women fall victim to various forms of destructive behavior, and the cycle of alienation worsens year by year. The more we undermine our natural institutions the harder it is to belong to a civilized order, and the more we will become tech-savvy barbarians. The answer is not better policy devised by lawmakers or bureaucrats, but rather a determination to refresh our collective memory of the family as our most natural and most intimate association – indeed, as the fundamental basis of an ordered, free society.

CHAPTER ELEVEN

Why We Need Religion

Religion is inescapable. Those who hope for religion's extinction and those who fear it both overlook a crucial fact of human nature: all of us are, by nature, religious animals. We all seek to make sense of our lives, and our deaths. Should we refuse to look above and beyond ourselves to God or the intrinsic structure of existence for answers to these questions, we will answer them in less wholesome ways, generally by assigning our will over to an ideology, to the state, or to our own passions. Moreover, any reasonably healthy religious faith must be lived within a community – we must join with others who share our vision of life's meaning in order to build any coherent life together. Lacking such commonality, we will be incapable of forming genuine communities, in which people associate on the basis of common beliefs regarding what is good, what kinds of behavior are required and forbidden, and what makes life worth living. Obviously, many casual associations (a rock-climbing or garden club, for example) are formed purely to facilitate individual activities and have no theological origin. But even these clubs exist within deeper, more formative communities that help people define who they are. The persons who make up these communities all seek meaning in their lives through common belief and action.

As sociologist Robert Nisbet pointed out, humans are by

nature communal animals. If we will not have healthy community, we will choose unhealthy communities. So also with religion. We will never escape the hold of religion. But if we neglect thinking about why religion is part of a healthy human life we will blind ourselves to the manifold ways that our need for religious meaning can take dangerous turns.

Americans remain a nation of believers: in a 2014 poll, 89 percent of respondents said they believe in God in the sense of a higher power (nearly two-thirds said their faith is "absolutely certain").* But elite opinion makers seem increasingly worried that people who act together on the basis of their faith are dangerous, would-be tyrants. As usual, the argument rests on a slippery slope; somehow a prayer offered at any sort of "official" event will lead to stigmatizing, then jailing nonconformists, then to Nazi book burnings, if not a holocaust. But it is precisely because religion is powerful that we should work to maintain its intrinsic links with our culture and way of life.

The Nazis denied the truth of the Christian as well as Jewish religions. They made Hitler and the Aryan race into false gods, deities in an ersatz religion, unhinged from moral reality and aimed at overturning the very nature of the human person, who is sinful yet worthy of love as a creature of God. Genuine religious communities were attacked and forced underground as all too many individuals became worshipers of the Nazi state. The same happened under communism in Stalin's Soviet Union and, most murderously of all, Mao's China. Religious communities were attacked, persecuted, forced underground, and murdered in unfathomable numbers, often in the name of

---

* Pew Research Center on Religion and Public Life, "Religious Landscape Study: Belief in God," 2014, http://www.pewforum.org/religious-landscape-study/belief-in-god/.

political ideology. Of course, there is no reason to think such horrors could happen in America. But a self-governing people should seek to protect the health of its religious communities because it is there that cultures and civilizations are made, and it is there that people learn the habits and build the associations necessary to limit the power and reach of the central government.

A distinction is important here: One's faith may be purely personal – a belief is something one has. But religion, a word deriving from a Latin root meaning "to bind," is a set of ordered beliefs and practices in which one engages as part of a group – a religion is central to who one is.

Religion – real, binding communities of faith and practice – constitutes a source of meaning and a form of life outside the state. This is what makes religion seem dangerous to those who want the state to help them transform society to fit their ideological vision. Where religion, as opposed to mere individual belief, holds sway, people will not look to directives from the government, whether delivered in public schools, through government agencies, or in administrative decrees and the law, for ultimate standards of right and wrong. Religious people recognize an authority higher than political power and so develop the courage and the means to stand up to political actors who would undermine their liberties and way of life.

Of course, self-governance is not simply a matter of standing up to political power; it requires that people develop the habits and associations of a self-governing people. This is the realm of culture. And culture is intimately related to religion. The word "cult" shares a Latin root with "culture" (and "cultivate"): both are related to shared practices that shape people's characters and their common ways of life. Where most secular Americans tend to think of religion as, at most, a weekly gathering of otherwise disconnected individuals, those of us who belong to strong religious communities know that religion includes active participation in religious celebrations, schooling, social outreach, caring for the less fortunate, and the variety of less formal interactions that make up a way of life. We live within cultures shaped by religious belief, standards of conduct, art, and attitudes about everything from education to commerce to personal honor.

Because a religion is a common tradition of action, religious principles like the Golden Rule are not just abstractions; they become real only when persons and groups put them into action within their local communities and thereby make them part of their ethos. Charity, civility, and the capacity (and desire) to be self-supporting are planted and nurtured through constant interaction in large things and small, interaction that motivates us to earn the approval of those with whom we share much of our lives. One can leave such communities and join others, or none. Ours is, after all, a country in which religious liberty, including the liberty to practice no religion, is held sacrosanct. But members of religious communities develop habits that help maintain our common life and the social, economic, and political lives of individual persons. We are all members of a variety of interlocking associations – family, town or region, workplace, local clubs and voluntary associations. Within such a community of communities, government has its place, but it is only one place among many, and not a commanding place: the state is just one source of authority among many, leaving all of us with the freedom to move among communities and even to strike out on our own to new lands to form new communities, as the West was won by people who had gained the habits necessary to forge new associations on established patterns wherever they went.

Religion binds not by law but by custom and friendship. Religious communities have the authority to guide behavior and correct bad conduct without calling on the potential violence of law and other state action. Indeed, religious communities teach their members how to build friendships within the church and outside it. They teach people the habits of association that they need to forge other communities and maintain peace and ordered liberty in the political sphere. Religion, then, is a locus of meaning and activity, a primary association whose influence helps shape all the other associations that give life meaning, and allow each of us to become fully human, both as individuals facing our God, and as members of functioning communities with common ends.

Those who fear religion claim they want to protect individual autonomy – to free each of us from the confines of binding structures and beliefs. But if we will not have the relatively soft structures of traditional religious communities, we will lose the habits and associations that build trust and habits of self-government. Then we will be left alone to face the state and the mass of the population, bereft of support, bereft of common meanings, with only power to determine who rules. If we will not have religious community, we will have ersatz community, rooted in an ersatz religion of the state, with all its potentially lethal power. This is the true inhumanity religion helps us prevent.

CHAPTER TWELVE

Community, Common Law, and Religious Association

As Tocqueville observed, Americans succeeded as a self-governing, democratic people because they managed to combine the spirit of religion with the spirit of liberty, as had no other nation on earth at the time. America was built on religious community. The Pilgrims bound themselves to one another and their God through a political compact, securing social order for themselves in an otherwise lawless New World. Frontier families in the West habitually established churches and hired ministers almost immediately after choosing a sheriff and building saloons. Churches, like law and gathering places to build new friendships, always were integral parts of new communities. No village was long without a church or a church building, which typically served as the place for public schooling and for town meetings. The symbolism of the church at the center of American acts of deliberation and self-rule can hardly be overstated. Americans made religion central to their public life. And this religiously rooted public life made possible the common ground for strangers to work together and become neighbors. Without self-organizing churches, America would never have developed its tradition of individual liberty in light of self-ruling communities.

America's early settlers often sprang from dissenting Calvinist communities in England whose members had "cove-nanted" with one another to cooperate and live godly lives together. As the Pilgrims' Mayflower Compact put it, members bound themselves before God "to enact, constitute, and frame such just and equal laws ... as shall be thought most meet and convenient for the general good of the Colony, unto which we promise all due submission and obedience." Whether in Plymouth Colony or the frontier West or points in-between, founding a township was a serious, communal act that meant forging anew the ties that tradition had set into members' hearts.

Townships' religious, governmental, economic, and civic institutions all overlapped in both membership and function. As a result, the township was an integrated whole that left much room for individuality and low-level conflict while forging common commitment to the common good. America's townships worked because they were in effect networks of local associations in which people ruled and were ruled in turn.

Each individual person was part of a variety of groups that shaped and gave purpose to that person's life. Two important "secular" elements, here, were scale and isolation. In face-to-face communities one learns that one will have to interact with others on a regular basis, which serves as an inducement to make that interaction relatively pleasant. In the negative sense, one cannot escape one's reputation if one chooses to be unhelpful, spiteful, or selfish. Moreover, when those face-to-face communities exist on the frontier, survival itself depends on cooperation; active voluntarism is not some hobby, it is both virtue and necessity.

The habit of voluntarism – of stepping forward to help clear that road, put out that fire, or take in that orphan – was not ingrained by mere necessity. History is full of instances where frontier peoples chose the path of communal failure by being selfish and cruel. American voluntarism was culturally, which is to say religiously, rooted. Voluntarism was not just a matter of sermonizing, though sermons there were, in church, in court, and from the office of mayor or sheriff. There was a rhythm and structure to life, with religious association and good works at its center. Public prayers, days of fasting and thanksgiving, church socials and festivals, churches' central location in the town, as well as church buildings' second role as meeting places, all bound members together and instilled the inclination to cooperate.

Americans in their communities shared a set of common assumptions about what made for a good life and what made for a good person. Common notions of virtue, of one's duties to oneself and the community, and of the community's duties to each person, allowed for social trust and civic friendship. People knew what to expect from one another; they understood their various roles in a shared common life. This is not the same thing as serfs who know their place in a fixed hierarchy. Conspicuously, American citizens were not serfs. American equality, as Tocqueville understood, meant that laws applied equally to all citizens, and, as important, each was part of various associations making up the community. Moreover, even among supposedly pliant Catholics, there was an emphasis on the individual person – created in the image of God, a full member of a parish or congregation, with complementary rights and duties – as well as on the community – a real, spiritual whole with its own personality and goals.

Long after American independence, there remained substantial institutional and even governmental supports for religion's central role in town life. School materials were unabashedly religious until well into the twentieth century. Ministers were respected members of the community, and often its leaders (though, in an early expression of separation of church and state, Puritan ministers were not allowed to hold public office in colonial New England). And the law was unabashedly moralistic. So-called blue laws enforced Sabbath observance. Laws against extramarital sex protected the family. Laws against vagrancy, public blasphemy, and public drunkenness guarded the civic square's role as a place for respectful engagement. The common law – that set of customs and usages enforced by courts, especially in cases of conflict – was deeply embedded in a Christian civilization that left much room for religious dissenters, members of differing religious communities, and the occasional atheist even as it steadfastly upheld common standards of public conduct.

Of course, the early republic had its problems. Corruption and low-level conflict regarding the nature of the common good and the limits of social control were common. Because our country always has respected the freedom to travel, the right to exit was important in maintaining both freedom and order. More disruptive was the influx of millions of Irish Catholics during the nineteenth century. Previously, a mix of compromise and separation had maintained townships' character. Different groups tended to form their own towns and, when circumstances brought them together in the same town, to split public support and emphasize common beliefs. Indeed, the American Constitution was written with this kind of unity-in-diversity in mind. That document steadfastly refused to take any position on state or local religious establishments, forbidding federal interference with religion in the states even as it approved federal promotion of religious education in the territories.

The Irish Catholic influx was different because of its size and because of longstanding ethnic and religious tensions. A number of important Protestant leaders sought to maintain their own overwhelmingly Protestant publicly funded schools while denying public support for Catholic schools. In the end, but not without much conflict, most localities forged working compromises by which Catholic schools received lesser forms of support for textbooks, student transportation, and the like. But the idea had been broached that public schools should be nonsectarian. While in most of America this meant only greater cooperation in matters like crafting public prayers, the idea of the separation of church and state – nowhere in our Constitution – gained institutional momentum with progressivism.

Only during the New Deal era did the Supreme Court "discover" that state and local government cooperation with religious associations somehow violates a federal Constitution specifically intended to preserve local arrangements. The Court took the most radical, sectarian view of religion available, that expressed by Thomas Jefferson in his Letter to the Danbury Baptist Association, and turned it into a false constitutional tenet. That sectarian view rests on the flawed assumption, found nowhere in our constitutional texts or traditions, that it is possible to separate persons' secular from their religious purposes, effects, and motivations.

Bound to this rabidly individualistic ideology, courts have set about determining what can be included in "holiday" displays, banishing prayer from public life, and marginalizing religious associations wherever possible. Court defenders sometimes argue that no rulings have actually required the more extreme forms of secularization, such as banning Christmas carols from public school concerts. But the courts have torn down and rebuilt our public square to make it hostile toward religion rather than reflecting our common commitments in the midst of our diversity. In the cause of protecting religious and irreligious minorities from possible discomfort or bad feelings, courts have sought to silence the voices of religious communities. The clear goal is to consign religious associations to a purely private sphere in which, for example, a religious school or charity will be left unmolested only if it employs, serves, and interacts with members of its own group, effectively withdrawing to a kind of Amish existence. Even here, devout persons who make their living as small-business owners may be compelled, despite the Supreme Court's 2018 ruling in the *Masterpiece Cakeshop* case, to participate through their art or craft in events, like same-sex weddings, in a manner that violates their religious conscience, provided the state is careful not to express clear animus against their faith in requiring them to do so. The courts increasingly police all our interactions to make certain no one is acting from "bad" motives – either too hostile or too friendly toward any particular religion. This leaves no room for either the spirit of religion or the spirit of liberty, the blending of which has been the peculiar American genius for self-rule and ordered liberty.

Most Americans (indeed, almost all, outside secular coastal enclaves) still live in communities where the remnants of religious community are wide and deep. Most everyone knows what the "holiday" display is really about. Public prayer continues whenever people think they can "get away with it." And the courts, so far, have left alone various forms of ceremonial deism, such as "in God we trust" on our currency and religious symbols in courthouses, on the thinly based theory that these symbols have lost their specifically religious meaning.

Perhaps more important as reminders of our lost home are the various church banquets, festivals, and charitable activities that remain important, especially in smaller towns. These social events continue to bind together people who share important beliefs and norms rooted in the divine. Marked on the family calendar, they shape Americans' social expectations and habits of interaction. They point to a tradition we have not yet fully lost. That tradition is nothing like the caricature of puritanical communities used to justify tearing us from our religious, legal, and civilizational moorings. It can be enlivened and rebuilt if we simply refuse to be cowed by the lawsuits and the courts that encourage them. The Supreme Court's hostility toward religion has infected many state courts and legislatures as well. But the American instinct for religious association remains strong. A return to true neutrality, especially at the federal court level, would allow for renewed sanity where it really counts. That sanity begins, as all else about which we have been writing, with a return to more local control.

CHAPTER THIRTEEN

Work and the Global Economy

Free markets are an important form of self-government among persons and businesses; they enable people to support themselves, their families, and others they care about, and to pursue their chosen vocations within the bounds of economic necessity. For these reasons, economic liberty is good and moral. It is deeply unfortunate that for so many decades moral discourse about economics has been dominated by various forms of socialists – those who would empower employees of the state to dictate to people where they should work, how they should work and for what compensation, and in the end how they should live their lives – all in the name of a notion of equality not as a basic presumption but the ultimate utopian goal.

For too long too many supporters of free markets have insisted on seeing them only in terms of economic efficiency (no small thing) and grand, idealized forces ("the market" and "creative destruction") or as a form of radical self-assertion. The defining purpose of economic activity is to provide material sustenance to make home possible. The English word "economy" derives from the Latin *oeconomia*, which in turn derives from the Greek *oikonomia*, meaning household management. Economics offers no end in itself but is good or virtuous to the degree that it sustains the family.

Economics by nature supports the larger purposes of human

life, which include taking care of physical needs, nurturing and providing security for family, contributing to community (working together toward common ends, whether teaching school or building a car or delivering a pizza), and supporting the leisure for what the social critic Christopher Lasch called "our common life." Other conventional purposes for economic activity – increased comfort, sense of achievement, and even social status – are good, so long as they do not undermine economics' defining purpose.

Of course, a free-market economy is impossible without rules. Central, here, is the protection of property. Economic liberty as developed in Western civilization depends on recognition that property is a natural right, and that labor or "work," which is the original moral basis of property, is necessary for human flourishing. People deserve the fruit of their labor and ought to be free to risk their property in pursuit of further gains so long as they do not impose the costs of their choices on others, including future generations. Governments, and courts especially, have important functions in facilitating private exchanges and protecting people's property and other natural rights from abusive conduct like fraud and intimidation.

Free markets, then, require government, but also keep government in the background, protecting rightful expectations about honest dealing rather than dictating outcomes. Socialism, on the other hand, places political actors in charge of planning economic production and distribution for politically determined ends. In the abstract, the contrast is clear and crucial. Unfortunately, today, the complicated geopolitical framework for global trade and production, created by treaties and transnational institutions as well as a host of technological innovations, offers none of the contrasting clarity of our inherited categories. Our struggle today to even name this new system, beyond the vague term "globalization," suggests the deeper problem. The term itself hides an astonishingly complicated set of political choices behind an ideology falsely claiming that changing the means of production inevitably produces parallel changes in all aspects of our lives. Economic materialism explains many things. But we cannot allow it to cloud our understanding of human choices made by those who benefit from changes in rules and laws. We cannot allow ourselves to accept the notion of an "arc of history" or self-serving claims of the "inevitability of progress"; these phrases are merely meant to suspend analysis and protect vested interests.

Should foreign companies, supported by government subsidies, be allowed to "dump" products below cost in American markets? Should we allow would-be workers to cross national borders at will, especially if this means supporting them with taxpayer funds? Such questions, along with issues related to protecting common resources and vulnerable people, show the necessity of prudence in dealing with economic (as with all other) issues. Unfortunately, in recent decades a simplistic form of libertarian ideology, often called neoliberalism and, as noted earlier, attacked by the left as a form of exploitative capitalism, has dominated economic arguments in both political parties. It has facilitated a second wave of globalization that is anything but pro-liberty, let alone conducive to a humane market economics.

Since the end of the Cold War, globalist ideology has rationalized the actions of governments and financial, technological, and industrial combinations with no loyalty to any nation, people, or community. This collusive set of elites has built a complex, cross-national structure of so-called free-trade agreements and financial arrangements enshrining their own power and economic interests in law and public policy. Shaping global markets into a tool by which they can build up and destroy local economies for their own ends, these elites have constructed a globalist system that is corrosive to all the natural institutions necessary to human happiness. The so-called free-trade agreements that rule so much of our economic lives are in fact multilateral deals to establish highly regulated zones of dominance for specific corporate entities, to be managed by globalist bureaucrats and financiers. They divide up wealth and markets in a fashion designed to benefit the powerful while leaving both industrializing nations and workers in nations already industrialized out in the cold.

Globalization's success relies in part on a sustained process of cultural forgetting. We already have observed that industrial capitalism, dating back at least to the early nineteenth century, has disrupted customs and traditions, bringing such rapid changes in people's ways of life as to blind them to historical continuity and their own cultural inheritance. This process has accelerated exponentially during our current second wave of globalization. Capitalizing on technological advances in financial administration, communications, and transportation, globalists from different walks of life but concentrated in finance, government, and high-tech have leveraged their expertise to bolster their own power and engage in radical efforts to transform human culture.

Before we can understand what contemporary globalization is doing to our culture, and what we should do about it, we first must remind ourselves of what is under assault given this new set of economic arrangements.

Americans tend to think of free markets as natural. They are correct in two important senses. First, free markets serve ends (sustenance, self-government, and leisure) that are important for any good life. Second, and related to the first, free markets are a full expression of the natural right to property. By "natural rights" we mean a set of moral obligations people owe one another regardless of whether some government imposes them through coercion. These rights have a deep history in Western civilization, going back at least to the first-century Roman thinker Seneca. Seneca insisted that certain natural laws exist prior to governmental power. The thirteenth-century Christian thinker Thomas Aquinas argued that the natural law refers to human moral ends, laid down in the nature of things by God, to which all of us, to fulfill our nature, ought to consent. Natural rights are little more than the form these ends take.

The idea of property as a natural right has roots in Catholic concerns with natural human needs but was developed especially by early Calvinists; it became central to Puritan thought and, through it, American economic assumptions. Crucial, here, was the importance of work. For Calvinists, nature (God's creation) was given equally to all. Private property (as opposed to the common property of unaltered nature) emerges when humans labor to improve nature's bounty.

Long before Locke wrote his *Second Treatise*, American Puritans based property rights on work. The Puritans saw unimproved land on which the Indians lived as available for acquisition by those who would apply their labor to it through cultivation or building. But this labor theory of value doesn't exhaust the moral importance of their theory. For these American Puritans, work was an extension of the person. One who labors does God's will, expressing himself in creative and productive ways.

Connecting property so intimately with the person's identity and purpose meant that his property was morally inalienable – no one had a right to it except by his consent. The implications of this natural rights view were far-reaching. The revolutionary issue of taxation without representation, for example, was not about fairness in taxation. It was about the right of a self-ruling people to control their own lives, liberty, and property.

The American struggle with property as a natural right was evident from the start of the nation: conflicts with Indian possessors (but nonimprovers) of the land; slavery, which is the ownership of both a person and that person's labor; federal ownership of vast tracts of land coveted by would-be farmers, ranchers, and tradesmen. All spurred efforts to maintain the material basis for the American ethic of self-support and self-government, from the "free soil, free labor" antislavery movement of the 1850s to homestead legislation.

The dynamics of American political and economic life sprang in large part from these conflicted circumstances. But the model of the independent yeoman relying on his own labor (and the labor of his household), participating in free government as a free, independent citizen, remained dominant in the American imagination all the way to the cusp of the industrial revolution. Two broad facts rendered this traditional view inadequate over time. First, industrialism brought change, involving countless financial, organizational, and technological innovations that were wide, deep, and rapid; they made it nearly impossible for inherited norms and expectations to make sense of the changing economic landscape. Second, industrial developments marginalized the "natural property" of the yeoman farm. Rather quickly, in historical terms, many, then most, farmers became employees. New means of production replaced traditional means of gaining wealth and finding reasonable economic independence.

The first industrial wave of globalization – roughly from 1870 until 1914 – produced a new form of economic interdependence. It connected almost all Americans in a web of abstract relationships among sources of capital (from banks to stockholders), corporate managers, suppliers, systems of distribution, and customers. Even small-town merchants and midwestern wheat farmers became enmeshed in international markets as they looked for supplies, labor, capital, and customers far outside their localities or even regions.

Among the last holdouts of economic independence and local autonomy were southern farmers who had been unable to modernize as had other farmers in the first part of the twentieth century. Even near-subsistence farmers in the South raised some tobacco, cotton, or other cash crop to sell in global markets, but they otherwise concentrated on growing what they ate, making what they wore, and living rather poorly but independently. As noted by historian Paul Conkin, the southern farmer in 1929, on the cusp of an agricultural revolution that would accelerate productivity at a greater pace than did the industrial revolution of the nineteenth century, lived and worked in ways more consistent with the farmer of 1800 than the farmer of 1960.*

New Deal programs changed all this. Expensive mechanized equipment, to cite one obvious example, spurred farm consolidation, pushing many out of farm life altogether. Huge farms using the newest pesticides, fertilizers, and equipment were able to produce single crops at low costs for widely flung markets. The small farmer selling a few dozen eggs at his local market for some spending money all but disappeared for decades.

By 1960 the transformation of American farming was complete. A much larger transformation had altered all aspects of

---

* Paul K. Conkin, *A Revolution Down on the Farm* (Lexington: University Press of Kentucky, 2008).

American life, creating what in many ways was a mass society. This was the trend in economics and culture that the Southern Agrarians, in the 1930s, and other traditionalists opposed. Some of these proponents of local community may have argued for a reactionary utopianism, but most recognized the genuine benefits of industrialization in relieving hunger and other forms of human misery. Traditionalists sought not to "undo" industrialization but to enliven the local communities in which Americans, by and large, still lived, and to resist a legal and administrative system that squeezed them into an inhumane, bureaucratic mold. The sometimes crushing uniformity of this system helped spur the political radicalism of the 1960s. Though leftist radicals of that era owed too much to mechanistic ideologies to address the key underlying problem, what they did accomplish was to further undermine respect for natural property rights even as mass industrialization weakened the norms and the local communities that, already under great stress, would be primary targets of globalization's second wave.

Since the late 1980s, second-wave globalization has undermined fundamentally the moral understanding of work, property, and the institutions necessary for a self-ruling people. No simplistic defense of capitalism or any other system can respond to the real issues of our time because the structure of our society has been compromised even as our economics has been dehumanized. If we are not to surrender to globalist elites we must understand that theirs was not merely some grand conspiracy to seize power; over time a wide variety of people remade our economic structures in ways that have reconfigured much of our society. The damage may be addressed – we can rebuild home. But to do so we first must understand the forces and reasoning that fight against us in this endeavor.

Among the necessary factors for first-wave globalization

were the amazing drop in transportation costs and increased reliability made possible by the steam engine. Ships and trains could move products more quickly and at lower costs and with greater predictability. Corporations that could use the newest technologies to produce more products at lower prices now had access to wider markets. In addition, laws and other factors that encouraged a freer flow of capital across national borders made it possible for corporations to secure the necessary investment to take advantage of these favorable transportation conditions. In the first wave of globalization, production remained fairly regional, but investment and sales became global.

Something similar but more dramatic has taken place since the late twentieth century. Information and communications technologies (to say nothing of advances in container shipping and other ways of lowering distribution costs globally) have allowed for a more radical and non-national structure to economic production. Corporations use these new technologies to escape the greatest limiting factor of the previous revolution: the concentration of highly productive workers and companies in specific, localized areas. Corporations now use cheap, instantaneous communications to monitor all the details of production from anywhere, enabling them to take advantage of cheap labor globally.

Western corporations farmed out production to local organizations from Bangladesh to China. Goods (or components) were produced for a fraction of the cost paid in already industrialized nations because of cheap labor and lax regulation, then shipped cheaply and reliably to anywhere in the world. Production costs related to infrastructure, health, and the environment were off-loaded to other parties – governmental or otherwise – as corporations became increasingly disconnected from place, nation, or any clear external system of regulation.

Second-wave globalization quickly produced recognizable benefits. Material well-being improved quickly, especially in developing nations. Consumers in developed nations were flooded with a cornucopia of cheap but glitzy goods. But the new system was not "free"; it was not open to choices by sovereign nations or the communities within them.

International agreements and treaties limited developing nations' abilities to capture some of the new wealth through taxes to pay for infrastructure improvements and the like. Intellectual property protections became draconian, limiting the ability of entrepreneurs to make use of new technologies. Supposedly liberal policies on tariffs (in fact a complex system of subsidies and cartelization that froze out less powerful players) limited countries' options in dealing with issues like dumping or predatory pricing.

A global system of production has helped the poorest parts of the world and brought untold wealth and enormous economic freedom to the top .001 percent of the world population. It also has undermined national sovereignty even as it makes all sources of labor vulnerable to the choices of corporations only marginally affected by political and legal rules. Workers in developed nations have been the biggest losers; their jobs have been lost in large numbers to overseas labor markets, and their political power to influence economic choices by the wealthiest corporations and individuals has reached an all-time low.

Second-wave globalization has produced a new oligarchy of high-tech so-called entrepreneurs (inaccurate since many of them depend for their start on government largesse) who operate virtual monopolies on the provision of electronic infrastructure and the distribution of goods, information, and entertainment. Proclaiming their devotion to social justice, these multibillion-aires ruthlessly exercise their economic power to reduce labor costs, destroy competition, and maintain outsized influence on public information and various governments' policies.

This is a system characterized by the insecurity of labor and a species of dependency that is outside the normal reach of political or social resources to resolve or change. No longer is control over one's labor the key to one's advancement in life or to one's ability to be secure and self-reliant. The nature of wealth has changed dramatically as it has been largely digitized and so flows unimpeded across almost all geographic lines.

From a conservative point of view, the resulting inequality of wealth is not in itself the problem. But the imbalances in power that come with this inequality corrode people's ability to take charge of their own lives and to live in community and relationship with others. We must, then, revisit conventional understandings about property and wealth, as well as their relationship with the political power of the community and the right of persons to have meaningful work to support a life of self-reliance.

Important responses to globalization already have taken shape. New microbusinesses, including farm-to-table marketing strategies for farms, stores, and restaurants, capitalize on the niche markets that grew up alongside globalization. Movements toward employee-owned companies continue but have faltered largely because current corporate structures prioritize short-term profits over long-term investment; still, they show a tendency toward business community and, especially, point to how badly we need to narrow the powers, benefits, and protections we give to those who own and manage stock.

The web of advantages woven into law and policy for globalist organizations needs to be unraveled. This means, to begin with, applying antitrust law to our massive high-tech monopolies. In addition, we must reduce the monopoly power that has grown up around intellectual property. Disney has "owned" the "right" to any and every portrayal of Mickey Mouse for quite long enough. The same goes for a whole host of patents, trademarks, and other protections of the rights of those who were first to file a new idea with the government. There simply is no rational, let alone moral, argument for allowing anyone to have a decades-long monopoly on the use of his or her idea or invention; this is especially true at a time when massive corporations are the ones funding, developing, and profiting from the vast majority of these (often quite small and technical) improvements in technology. Excessive protection of ideas as property undermines the ability of small businesses to compete and grow.

It also is crucial to recognize the genuine roles that belong to national governments. The national state is a community of communities. To say so is in no way to retreat from our insistence on the importance of restoring federalism and the centrality of the township. Nations have an essential role to play in defending their people – both militarily and economically. Governments have the right and the duty to defend their nation's economic well-being as much as national security; they have no right to push authority and power off to a distant elite with its own parochial (intentionally mislabeled global) interests.

Finally, and perhaps most importantly, nations have a duty to protect their borders for the sake of their economic well-being and as a means of maintaining their national character and the character of their specific, local communities. It is to this duty that we turn next.

CHAPTER FOURTEEN

Defining the People
Borders and Immigration

O ne thing a national government must do, if it is to serve its purpose in any meaningful sense, is protect its borders. Preventing invasions is the most basic, fundamental require- ment of a nation's government. Globalists, of course, are not supporters of the nation in any meaningful form; for them a nation is a collection of individuals who happen to live in a spe- cific area on the map designated as belonging to a specific gov- ernment. As to that government, globalists are concerned to reduce as much as possible its interference in the international movement of all elements of production, from capital, to goods, to labor inputs – what we would call people – while seeing that as many costs as possible are borne by the people and govern- ments of these nations.

Neoliberal globalists are not the only ones who reject the legitimacy of national borders. Leftists of various sorts argue that open borders are demanded by "American values," which seems to mean individual autonomy – the right of any person to go wherever that person wants – and, more in the back- ground, a duty to equalize global material conditions by extend- ing American government benefits to anyone who can make it across our borders.

For decades now, most supporters of prudent immigration

policies have been all but silenced by the charge that their core arguments – our duty to protect our own workers, our own way of life, and our national character – are somehow racist. But these principles do not rest on any false genetic theory. And abandoning our principles in the face of false charges has allowed bad policies to harm our national character and the millions of workers whose economic interests have been sacrificed in the name of global equality.

To speak of national character is simply to recognize universal facts of human nature. We all share the same God-given nature. That nature is intrinsically social and historical. We are born into, reared within, and live in communities, from the family to the neighborhood, the city, and the state. We are immersed throughout our lives in the institutions, beliefs, and practices – as well as the personalities – that shape who we are. Not only the necessity of those institutions but their formative power requires that we focus on them as the primary means of creating the social and cultural solidarity that makes possible the political life of self-ruling people.

Among the essential goods of any community is its identity. Nations, even nations made up of persons and communities that are, in historical terms, relative newcomers, have a character derived from the characters of their people. One often hears that America is a land of immigrants and that there is no particular American character beyond adherence to principles of freedom and equality and, perhaps, a tendency toward independence or individualism. But America was settled at least as much by communities (some of which immigrated wholesale to the New World) as by individual persons. And the cultural origins of American society lie clearly and deeply in the Judeo-Christian tradition, the towns and villages of Great Britain, and the commercial habits of "the middling sort" who made up the bulk of its first elites. As other immigrants have come to our shores, they have enriched our character and way of life precisely because their members worked to become fully American. Each new wave of immigrants found an already established order: legal, social, cultural, moral, and even aesthetic. But in each new wave immigrants both incorporated themselves into this settled order and added to American civilization in diverse and generally positive ways. As we noted near the outset of our history, the Anglo-American way of developing norms is by way of deep experience rather than abstract reasoning. Every social and cultural addition became part of the great web of American experiences, inflecting society while also being incorporated into a living tradition.

None of these cultural facts justifies an immigration policy that excludes on the basis of false genetic assumptions. Nor do these facts justify closing America's doors to those fleeing oppression. Our traditions, and humanity itself, dictate generosity in dealing with the refugee. But they do not dictate, indeed they argue against, policies that would erode or eliminate the character of the communities that make up the United States. Our personal duty to extend mercy to the refugee must be exercised within a nation that has primary duties of maintaining the safety, integrity, and economic well-being of the communities that constitute it. As to immigration, there is no inherent right to settle wherever one wishes, only the desire to relocate and the need for both the would-be immigrant and the potential host society to determine in good faith whether a specific person's immigration will serve the interests of everyone involved – but most especially the interests of the host society's preexisting communities. To claim otherwise is to privilege ideology over the real interests and dignity of actual persons.

Unfortunately, current immigration policies emerge more

from ideology than from principles engendered and modified by generations of experience. These policies emphasize cultural randomness regarding legal immigration, politically correct attitudes regarding refugee asylum, and sheer hypocrisy (to say nothing of political opportunism) in our dealings with illegal immigrants.

The current immigration regime, put into place in 1965 in legislation sponsored by Senator Ted Kennedy, did away with policies aimed at protecting Americans' interests and maintaining their way of life, even as those older policies made room for many people who had the means and determination to contribute to that way of life. The former rules recognized that people from different nations develop different norms, customs, and traditions, and that some of those are more easily assimilated into American culture than others. Today, this recognition of basic human nature and historicity – both empirical truths about the human condition – makes one a racist in the abstracting gaze of ideologues. The immigrant, in the mind of such ideologues, is an individual like any other – a bundle of ahistorical drives, desires, and rights, including the right to move and access government benefits wherever it wishes.

A principled immigration policy must match conditions for immigration with the needs and goods of the nation. Central, here, is the requirement that immigrants come with skills and the means to support themselves. Such requirements serve the needs of the host nation and even better serve the needs of migrants, who thereby can participate meaningfully in the American story of a self-ruling people.

One of the (far from principled) strategies used by advocates of expansive immigration is support for the policy of family reunification. As conservatives, we recognize the centrality of the family in the formation of any decent culture or character.

However, in America in particular, there are limits on the family's calls on our loyalty. Those limits include adherence to law and recognition of the competing interests of other associations. It is one thing, therefore, to insist that an immigrant be allowed to bring his immediate family over with him, especially once he is settled; but family reunification has been applied to cousins, grandparents, and other more distant relatives with dubious justification. Such distant relations must earn their own way into the American nation. No sane, competent nation can take in mass numbers of immigrants who lack the financial and educational resources and the determination to fit in with its own way of life and to become active, productive contributors to it. This way lies national suicide.

We cannot simply revert to our old immigration system. But we must reclaim control over our borders, along with our determination to choose who comes here based on their ability and willingness to become fully American in the best sense. This means choosing to allow in and naturalize immigrants only if they have skills necessary to our economy. It means exercising caution when looking to allow in would-be immigrants who come from cultures significantly different from our own, especially when it comes to fundamental institutions like the family, duties toward strangers, and adherence to the rule of law. It means that, while America always has been quite open-minded, historically speaking, to religious differences, those who seek to immigrate must recognize that they must leave behind religious strictures that impose legal cultures, marriage structures, or attitudes toward public morals that are at odds with American liberty.

Whatever progressives and leftists may claim, our culture, our legal system, and our ways of dealing with one another in the public square are shaped fundamentally by Christian conceptions of public decorum, the limitations of self-help, and a whole host of rights and duties commonly dismissed as manners but quite important for immigrants to learn if we are to maintain public order. It is no insult to any person or community to note that they are not all alike, and that they have their own character, identity, and integrity. But this means that not all communities are capable of living together in the full sense of becoming one and the same community. Sometimes political and/or geographical distance is an aid to friendship and understanding because it keeps certain fundamental issues (e.g., monogamy vs. polygamy) from becoming relevant to everyday interaction.

Moreover, and too often lost in cultural arguments, our national government owes it to the American people to protect their economic interests. This means not only screening would-be immigrants to make sure they are capable of supporting themselves but also refusing to allow in workers – whether temporary or permanent – who will take jobs away from Americans. The problem, here, includes skilled workers like computer engineers. Tens of thousands of foreign workers are being used by corporations (especially in the high-tech sector) to suppress wages and maintain unfair bargaining power regarding working conditions. Skilled foreign workers are brought over on the condition that they retain their specific jobs. To be fired from their company is to be fired from the United States. This is reasonable from a national point of view – we don't want people staying if they've proven they can't hold down a job. But this also empowers employers to make these employees' working conditions all but unbearable because they in effect have no right to complain. And that means increasing pressure on American employees to accept lower wages and go along with whatever management wants for fear of being replaced by such indentured workers.

The situation is far worse where unskilled and especially illegal immigrants are concerned. Far from opening our arms to these people, we are doing them no favors when we allow them to stay on condition that they accept second-class status. Businesses that hire immigrants with guest-worker status in a real sense control their fate. The saddest are those who enter illegally, hoping for an amnesty down the road. In the meantime, they serve as menial workers, doing as they are told in impoverished conditions. Their children come to see America as a land of opportunity for some, but for them a land of fear and poverty. All this is to be endured in hopes that they or their children may be granted citizenship by some distant political figure who does not answer to them.

We are not attempting to whitewash very real problems presented by illegal immigration – the drain on public services, the refusal to assimilate, and crime. We are pointing to a different but equally important problem: a system that makes their presence illegal yet tolerates it encourages dysfunction and resentment. We should not expect people waiting for amnesty to love a system that lets them into the country and then denies them the protection of its laws. Our current immigration mess can only breed cynicism concerning the ways in which our governments dole out services, social welfare funds, and even access to justice. People should not be treated as second-rate persons. The answer is to stop giving amnesties, to stop allowing people to enter the country illegally and stay, and most important to stop allowing employers to get away with knowingly hiring illegal immigrants. Real, meaningful fines combined with real protection of our borders would allow for development of a sensible immigration program.

It takes no deep reflection to recognize that our character as persons and the character of our communities are shaped by circumstances ranging from geographical location to religious tradition to historically rooted economic practices. It is no less clear that our universal rights and duties are made real only when they are made concrete, through experience with the particular. Every nation has a duty to protect the well-being of its member communities. It has other duties as well. One might posit that it is a nation's duty to welcome immigrants, but to prioritize that abstract ideal above the concrete duty to protect one's own is to denigrate the relationships that make us fully human in favor of an ideological vision that cannot be fulfilled.

No nation or society can survive if its people do not share common norms and the mutual trust that grows from them. We have been losing these common norms, in part because our national government has not been doing its job of protecting our borders. The answer to this particular problem is evident: prudent immigration policies backed up by effective enforcement. A sensible immigration system would benefit our culture and would help the many workers who, even in prosperous times, find themselves without jobs, unable to demand fair treatment from their employers, or forced to accept unfair treatment because they can't change jobs.

CHAPTER FIFTEEN

How We Can Stop Hating Our Public Schools

Why do conservatives hate public schools? Reasons are legion: early childhood sex education programs focusing on how-to guides provided by Planned Parenthood and featuring anal sex; textbooks that present a one-sided picture of America as racist, sexist, and homophobic; zero-tolerance policies bringing suspension or expulsion of children "caught" pretending ordinary objects (in one notorious case, a Pop-Tart) are guns; disciplinary policies punishing disruptive behavior with suspension or expulsion of some students but not others, strictly on the basis of race. All this and a huge bureaucracy that dehumanizes parents, warehouses children, and produces epic failures in educating for life and higher learning. But these abominations are just the tips of a very large, deep iceberg spawned from the cold waters of centralized power. These waters are fed by an ideology that disparages history, traditional values, and local control in favor of a system in which children are treated as chunks of clay, separated from any nurturing source in family and neighborhood, to be shaped by "experts" into pliant parts of a progressive national community.

Unfortunately, many of the supposed cures for this situation are simply forms of the disease itself. In recent decades, programs like President George W. Bush's No Child Left Behind aimed to bring quality control to the increasingly nationalized education system but merely added yet another layer of bureaucracy for delivering failure. Understandably, more and more Americans are choosing to take their children out of public schools in favor of private, parochial, and home schooling. But those most in need of educational reform – poor kids in inner-city neighborhoods – don't have the means of escape. And programs such as school choice and charter schools, while of potential use, threaten to further empower national elites even as educrats work to re-regulate private and even home schooling.

Programs like school choice too often aim at the wrong problem. The "choice" provided by government-controlled markets is largely illusory. Whatever may be on the menu in terms of curricular emphasis (arts or science, for example), if we leave education in the hands of administrators and teachers trained to enforce the rules and ideology of a distant bureaucracy we will achieve very little. Moreover, the problem with public schools is not that they are public, in the sense that they serve and are responsible to an identifiable public. The problem is precisely that they are run by people and according to rules that are too distant from, and consequently hostile toward, our local communities.

For hundreds of years, local schooling in America thrived and helped form the culture and traditions that shaped our people. Both the idea and the practice of public education predate the republic itself. The first publicly funded school in America was founded in 1635. Throughout New England, towns and villages set up primary schools beginning in the mid-seventeenth century.

Whether in settled cities or on the frontier, schools in America were self-consciously local affairs. Parents and town elders found a teacher and a building to serve as a school. Sometimes there was formal government support; funding might come from local taxes, local philanthropists, or school fees.

Always there was a concern to help children become productive members of their own communities. Acknowledging that some would have the desire, talent, and drive to go elsewhere, those who started and ran the schools saw admission to full membership in the community at the center of education.

Today, politicians, professional educators, and administrators all tell us that the federally regulated public school is essential to American public life – that it is the place where children from widely divergent socioeconomic, racial, and ethnic backgrounds come together to learn what it means to be an American. It is understandable that conservatives hark back to this vision as they face an education establishment determined to undermine our common culture. But we need to remember that, historically, American schools integrated students not into some national community defined by ideology but into local communities defined by tradition, history, and local relationships.

Nationalized education got its start with the famous nineteenth-century educator Horace Mann. Mann declared that immigrants would be taught to be Americans, and Americans would be taught to be good citizens, in schools where professional educators instructed students in an American civil religion. Important elements of this program included teaching children about their cultural and intellectual patrimony, their nation, and their civilization. Despite this nod to traditionalism, however, Mann was, in fact, dramatically changing the form of schooling within American localities, to say nothing of the prejudice he fostered against religious and ethnic minorities – especially those from Ireland.

In Mann's time, massive numbers of impoverished Irish Catholics were immigrating to the United States. Like many Americans, Mann had a rational fear that large numbers of poor ethnics from a distinctly minority religion would harm the American character. Unfortunately, instead of working within American traditions, activating local associations, and promoting sufficient local schooling, he and his allies sought to turn local schools from reflections of preexisting, local culture into institutions aimed at fitting children for a broader, more politicized national culture. Worse, the same people who demanded this expanded role for schools successfully fought recent immigrants' attempts to gain local funding for their own schools. The result, unfortunately, was an emptying out of religion from public schools, along with a more general shift in schools' functions, handing over power to professional educators concerned more with training national citizens than with teaching members of local communities. Over time, this shift took schooling away from Americans' culturally rich and diverse local communities and replaced it with a homogenized system, controlled by distant bureaucrats, that undermines local self-rule and erodes local culture.

The nationalization process took decades and has never fully succeeded in stamping out local culture from all our schools. But it has brought an overall system that is destructive of community, education, and individual character.

There are clear elements necessary for full membership in the American tradition – principally acceptance of our basic model of moral life: faith, family, and freedom culminating in a life of self-reliance within active communities and the behavioral norms of our common law traditions. But few of these elements can be taught by professional educators in schools isolated from their communities; they require assimilation through daily interaction with people and associations making up a local life. The attempt to teach them didactically turns these norms into an ideology – a set of abstract, pat answers to complicated questions that amount to political indoctrination instead of genuine learning.

One of the most significant consequences of education's nationalization has been the damage done to the set of associations, from school boards to parent-teacher associations to community foundations, that once thrived in the United States. Now shackled by national requirements and the constant pursuit of federal dollars, local school systems have become among the most corrupt institutions in America. With few substantive issues to debate, local school boards spend tens of millions of dollars on unneeded vanity projects, lining the pockets of favored businesses while virtue signaling and handing over real power to corrupt union officials and soulless educrats.

The real solution to our public education problem is a return to local control, which is to say to public accountability. This will be difficult, especially because local educational infrastructure has become so worn down and corrupt. Reform's first essential step will bring shock and resistance because it means ending federal and even state control over local education. Genuine participation and accountability require eliminating tax support, including support provided through state equalization schemes that purport to make education more fair by redistributing tax money from one district to another. Only if citizens of specific, small districts are in charge of raising *and paying* the funds they then decide how to use will it be possible to reestablish the kind of local parental involvement essential to schools' again becoming embedded in their communities. Only in this way can we fully eliminate state and national control that insulates teachers and educrats from parents and community leaders. Only in this way can we rebuild the self-confidence and mutual trust necessary to support children in their drive to become educated members of their communities.

The sky will not fall if local communities reclaim responsibility as well as control over local education. We know, for example, that school districts spending the most per student often are the least successful in educating those students. Programs aimed at replacing broken families with politically correct programming perpetuate failure and resentment. Opportunities for local associations and families – including single-parent and other struggling families – to genuinely participate in their children's education provide the only means by which communities and lives can be rebuilt and children set on the way to success in their jobs and, even more important, in their communities.

CHAPTER SIXTEEN

From Indoctrination to Education
Salvaging the University

The promise of higher education has become a trap for tens of millions of Americans. The promise: every one of us and our children could go to college, earn a degree, and set off on a good career, secure in the knowledge that we had gained the tools necessary for a productive life. The trap: years (usually more than the advertised four) of indoctrination in the classroom and, more harshly, the dormitories, followed by decades of crushing debt, all made far worse by the realization that our degrees have qualified us for very little.

It wasn't always like this. Supporters of the current system may argue that early colleges were mere playgrounds for the rich, but they were in fact set up for a variety of reasons – most of them having to do with training ministers and teachers. Few could afford college, and few needed to attend college to pursue a useful profession. Still, many men of talent (Alexander Hamilton, for example) were helped by generous friends and neighbors to pursue higher education. For much of American history, college was an opportunity for privileged young people to gain an understanding of their traditions and of the great works of their civilization, as well as for significant numbers of talented but not privileged young people to gain that same understanding as they worked their way into the learned professions.

Historically, higher education was an extremely costly enterprise. As a frame of reference, worldwide GDP per capita remained remarkably constant at about $500 (in 1990 dollars) for well over two thousand years.** Scarcity was the rule everywhere. Thus higher education in any society before the nineteenth century had to focus primarily on its most essential purpose: preserving knowledge, art, and, in sum, inherited culture. While universities always have been places where scholars pursue new knowledge, their first task has been to preserve civilization by passing down cultural and intellectual resources to the few who will hold positions of sufficient power for them to preserve and enrich it, or destroy it.

New possibilities for a university emerge when a society can devote more money and release people from productive labor (particularly the production of food and essentials) for more years. American higher education emerged in tandem with three powerful trends: (1) previously unknown and widely distributed wealth (GDP in America increased tenfold between the mid-eighteenth and mid-nineteenth centuries, then spiked even faster); (2) the rise of democratic impulses for equality of opportunity; and (3) the modern acceleration of technological change, with its demand for ever new and increased technological skills. In response to these circumstances, American higher education took on new purposes. At first continuing its civilizational purpose, universities began to stress the acquisition of new knowledge. In addition, higher education was expanded in scope and availability out of a desire both to prepare people to make a living and to educate them for citizenship. In a democracy, of course, every person is supposed to be informed

---

** Known as the Maddison benchmark. See Angus Maddison's historical statistics at the Groningen Growth and Development Centre, http://www.ggdc.net/maddison/.

and knowledgeable about the world because each person is involved in a deliberative political life. As the world became more complex, access to more education seemed appropriate to maintain the quality of American self-rule.

The new focus on higher education during the nineteenth century was undertaken in a spirit of community voluntarism. Improvement-minded communities founded hundreds of small colleges. Unlike higher education today, the result was not an integrated system. Politicized accrediting agencies didn't dictate what could be taught and how. Instead, a stunning variety of institutions and methods grew up to meet the needs of various communities. From teachers' colleges to divinity schools, to liberal arts colleges and the first law schools, institutions were fashioned to meet the emerging needs of their communities. Each local and usually private institution was both a repository of Western civilization and a preparatory ground for a useful life in a politically and economically dynamic world.

Public universities were an increasingly important part of the mix, especially after the Civil War, when the federal government encouraged the founding of land-grant colleges aimed at improving agricultural techniques. Some public schools mimicked preexisting private universities in their attempts to expand knowledge in a wide variety of endeavors. But most saw their purpose, as with so many of the smaller private colleges, as preparing their own people to help their communities.

Higher education in the twenty-first century bears little resemblance to this American way of educating. In the space of a short chapter, we cannot offer even a rudimentary account of this complex transformation. We must note, however, the importance of the federal government's decision to subsidize universities during World War II and the Cold War to secure technological and military advances. In addition, changes in the sorts of knowledge necessary for economic success during the second half of the twentieth century changed incentives to attend college, along with university curricula. Motivated by a deep presentism, American universities soon deemphasized or dropped higher education's first, civilizational purpose in favor of empowering individuals with knowledge necessary to meet their needs of the moment.

Over the last half-century, the dominant trends in American universities have been in two directions. The first has been to advance the quality, reach, and applicability of expert knowledge. Increasingly, a degree was supposed to signify deep competence in some narrow field of knowledge rather than the sort of knowledge once considered necessary for a free and self-governing society. The second trend has been to liberate the individual from institutions, traditions, and even norms or expectations that might hamper the self-creation and self-expression now deemed everyone's birthright. Rather than inhabiting and participating in a long civilizational story, the liberated student of today is expected to make his or her own story. Higher education now aims to produce highly trained idiots (in the original Greek, the word meant a private person) who function in an economic system they cannot comprehend, defer to a government that protects their radical individualism, and, as deracinated global citizens, define their moral universe through abstract notions of equality and justice.

Few who are not themselves part of the problem need to be told that our current university system is in shambles. Free inquiry has been replaced by "safe spaces" and the shouting down of anyone who speaks out against anti-Western ideologies and the cult of victimization. Bureaucracies that smack of the old Soviet Union enforce a code of political correctness infusing every aspect of university life with suspicion and resentment. Having banished all but a tiny remnant of conservatives and even most liberals from the professoriat, universities become ever more determined to undermine all aspects of American culture and higher learning. Culturally and intellectually, the moral objective of American universities is transformational rather than formative – they seek not to preserve, improve, and pass down but to destroy and build anew. Even the sciences have become targets of an irrational hostility toward reality; as students in some engineering education courses are told, for example, the skills necessary to, say, build bridges that will not collapse are tainted by racism, sexism, and homophobia.

Much has been written on the depth and breadth of the disaster that is American higher education today. We are less concerned with rehearsing the damning evidence than with suggesting a response in keeping with conservative principles. Most relevant, here, is the duty of all associations – including those engaged in higher education – to seek the public good. Educational institutions must aim to improve their communities by preparing their young people to become full, productive members – to be better citizens, better neighbors, better spouses, and better parents. These institutions must be an expression of their communities while offering the special cosmopolitanism of a liberal education, in the breadth and depth of tradition and history.

Because our primary and secondary education has declined so far in its ability to prepare young people for productive lives, many of them look to college to complete what is basically vocational training. It is crucial that our communities do a better job training young people to become good carpenters, welders, or clerks. To do well in skilled trades and many other jobs does not require, and should not be made to require, the investment of four or more years and tens of thousands of dollars in university degrees, especially when those degrees are drenched in left-wing ideologies.

This is not to say that universities, and especially liberal arts colleges, have no place in our society. All of us are participants in the continuing story of civilization – the literary, artistic, scientific, historical, and political traditions of the West, and of America. Our flourishing depends on proper education in these traditions. The liberal arts, now the realm of formless postmodernism, once provided a solid foundation of knowledge for a relatively small number of people who sought to become professionals or to make cultural and intellectual pursuits a central part of their lives. Even during this earlier era, however, most Americans recognized that this genuinely liberal education was important to everyone, and it was thus provided at home and in primary and secondary schools. Today, the claim that everyone should have a liberal arts or any other fully immersive university education is little more than a cynical argument for pressuring all our young people into the increasingly hostile and useless halls of academe. In the 1960s, radicalized youth mocked a diploma as just a piece of paper. In our time, leftist academia has in many cases proved them right.

The problem is not simply that our universities have been taken over by bad actors. The problem is that it is impossible for *any* national university system to serve the common good. To reclaim higher education for our culture, and for its own proper ends, it must again be the product of local communities serving local needs. We are not saying that the large research university should be abolished. But it is long past time for American taxpayers to stop supporting its maintenance, let alone its expansion. We currently spend billions of dollars subsidizing a system that rewards ideological malpractice, seeking to undermine our way of life as it enriches a few top administrators, enables self-indulgence among all too many professors, allows educrats to hector and indoctrinate our young people, and fails to serve our common interests.

Obviously enough, reform must take at least two paths, one dealing with private universities, the other with public ones.

First, where private universities are concerned, we often are told that what they do is a matter of purely private concern. Being privately funded, the argument goes, these universities have a right to teach whatever they want to whomever they want, charging as much as they want. In a sense this is true; but, as with much else, national political structures have brought a concentration of power into the wrong, politicized hands. Federal subsidies in the form of accrediting agencies that keep out genuine competition, grants, loans, special tax treatment, and government research funds all enable powerful universities to ignore their duties to their students while working to undermine the society that supports them.

Private universities have loaded up on administrative positions, launched tendentious, anti-intellectual academic programs, and engaged in counterproductive agitation in large part because they need not worry about the costs. However large the tuition hikes, students and their parents are lured into taking on massive, subsidized debt in the belief that college is "worth it," provided the school has a high-enough ranking. Competing only with one another, and only in the eyes of accrediting agencies and other gatekeeping institutions that share their own ideological views, colleges can stock their curriculum with classes in various forms of postmodern ideology and identity politics, seldom worrying about whether graduates will be able to find meaningful employment, let alone flourish as full members of their communities. Indeed, universities increasingly ignore altogether their duty to teach students because government contracts and research grants provide them with so much prestige and money. Most students, then, are coddled but not educated, trained in resentment not critical thinking, taught to despise their traditions rather than to enrich them.

The good news regarding private universities is that the prudent, reasonable solution to our problem is rather simple: stop the subsidies. We are not, and should not be, in a position to force sudden change on private universities – and certainly not through national political action. That said, we can and should stop funding a model of education that is financially profligate and culturally destructive. How can this be accomplished? Ending federal grants and loans, or at least capping at a level well below current tuition charges, will encourage a return to fiscal discipline. Eliminating subsidies for research, or at least insisting that it be done in independent facilities, will refocus universities' attention on teaching. Ending remaining exemptions on our huge university endowments, or at least requiring that the monies be spent regularly on university activities, will reconnect administrators with the students they are supposed to serve. Taken by themselves, these reforms will not return private universities as a class to cultural sanity. They will, however, provide much more room for conservative principles to be heard on college campuses and for conservatives, in combination with open-minded liberals, to restore an openness to honest inquiry and exchange of ideas capable of enlivening university life.

Where public universities are concerned, it is long past time for state legislatures to reassert public educational institutions' duty to serve their particular communities and the public good, not the desires of accreditors, administrators, and faculty. Nor should public universities gear their mission to students' whims as expressed in short-sighted surveys or protests. We are advocating not overt politicization of public universities but the opposite: these schools for too long have been allowed to become dens of radical politics precisely because they have lost sight of their intrinsic purpose – to help young people become ready for lives and careers within their communities.

Public universities are specifically set up, using public funds, for the good of the people of their state. The huge public research university, mimicking Ivy League colleges in every way possible while ignoring the needs of its state and local communities, is a travesty. These enormous institutions have hijacked public funds and the very idea of a public trust to serve their own financial interests, in large measure by claiming to serve a "public" that is global, ahistorical, and bereft of substantive interest or identity. Even smaller public colleges today seek freedom from public duty by claiming to serve everyone and every good thing.

Public colleges and universities must be reoriented locally. How is this to be done? To begin with, most public colleges have enforceable charters that are poorly drafted and often ignored; these could be rewritten and enforced by boards of trustees and, more likely, state legislatures. State legislators bow too easily to the charge of philistinism when they seek to fulfill the duty to oversee the institutions they fund. If there is to be public funding, there must be a determination that such funding support institutions that focus on the people of their own state in hiring, admissions, and curriculum. This last means that it is the duty especially of regional institutions to provide the kinds of vocational training that currently falls through the cracks, picked up neither by community nor regional colleges. Budget discipline also can be used to slash the number of administrators currently pushing programs of political and cultural transformation on campus as well as the tuition students must pay.

The solution to the breakdown of university education is not further control from Washington. Improvement in education, as in most things, is to be found through decentralization and rethinking at the more local level. As universities have claimed to be all things to all people, they have become, intellectually and culturally speaking, less than nothing. Meanwhile, our children increasingly are told that their choices are lifetimes of debt or lifetimes of ignorance and unskilled labor. We can and must eliminate this false choice by freeing higher education from the grips of a national establishment concerned with its own material and ideological interests so that the real interests of persons and communities can be recognized and served.

America's Three Contracts

We began this book stressing experiences rather than ideas. In particular we noted widespread anxiety and the disorienting feeling of living in a time when "all that is solid melts into air." This evocative phrase, written by Marx in 1848, expresses the defining modern experience of spiritual homelessness that brought ideology and unprecedented violence to Europeans. While America was spared from this radical modernity for most of our history, it has become the primary threat to our American home.

Unprecedented technological, social, intellectual, and cultural change over the past two centuries has undermined the conditions necessary for rooted, tradition-oriented people to connect to a larger story. In Europe and parts of Asia, the resulting unscriptedness, which robbed so many people of comforting and defining social roles, also destroyed familiar moral signposts and undermined heretofore unquestioned truths. These "acids of modernity," as Walter Lippmann put it in 1929, dissolved the sources of people's truest identity.* Feeling alien – homeless – in their own lands, many peoples of Europe turned for security and purpose to radical ideologies. The madness of these ideologies led to horrific wars and holocausts on a scale

---

* Walter Lippman, *A Preface to Morals* (New Brunswick, NJ: Transaction, 1982).

that shocks us to this day. Spiritual and cultural homelessness, in short, produced the most destructive, nihilistic movements in human history – so far.

But not in America. Why not? A central reason for our people's social and cultural stability and relative health has been the salutary role played by the American conservative tradition. American conservatism offers no utopian vision, no presumed golden age, and no ideological system. We cannot overstate how important this has been to the success of the American tradition of self-rule. Both the left and the right in Europe offered ideologies to feed their masses – a mass being what becomes of a people that is homeless and alienated. American conservatism, meanwhile, offered tradition, prudence, and experience as both the tools and the measure of successful adjustment to changing circumstances. The institutions that house the conservative soul survived because they rise from the ground up. The natural formations of family and religion as well as civic institutions and associations – schools, Little Leagues, clubs, and gatherings – both shaped and reflected the self-reliant character emerging out of the American experience.

And yet America's conservative soul, after a century of abuse and unprecedented challenges, is threatened and increasingly isolated from its animating conditions and resources. In our current homeless condition, Americans are more likely than ever before to heed the siren call of ideology and ersatz community that hide from us our true nature. The attraction of progressivism is a logical, if dangerous, symptom of our present cultural fragility. When all the orienting connections to family, neighbor, community, and generations past and future are severed, we become spiritually disoriented and morally hungry. This spiritual hunger can deform a people so that only a comprehensive and compelling vision of justice seems to offer answers. Our hunger makes us vulnerable to the palliative of ideology. Under the unyielding moralism of ideology, we reject both our history and the society it created because they are imperfect. The inevitable inequalities and injustices of life no longer motivate us to alleviate suffering and address abuses, but rather to rage against abstract entities we are told stand in the way of a notion of social justice that in truth is unachievable and ultimately inhumane.

In this book we have told the story of America as seen in its conservative tradition. We have argued for the necessary relationship between experience and principle while seeking to set out and defend principles we know are suited to our nature as humans who belong to the American story. And we have called on Americans to reclaim the longer and more useful conservative tradition from those who have turned it into a simple ideology born out of Cold War circumstances.

The problems we face are neither so intractable nor so inevitable as we have been led to believe. The American story of a self-ruling people supports, as it is informed by, two distinctly American intellectual and cultural traditions – the liberal and the conservative. The dynamic tension between these two traditions is natural and healthy in our society. It is only the emergence of a species of leftism that we call progressivism that has seriously threatened the shared American story. Progressives do not seek to reform or improve according to prudential limits. Progressives want to transform America – to destroy what it is and make it anew according to their vision of justice.

America is entering a time of choosing similar to what Europeans faced in the late nineteenth through mid-twentieth centuries – except that Americans have the deep experiences of self-rule and the resources and tradition of American conservatism to guide us. We may seek to impose an ideological vision –

a second, simplified, and fundamentally false reality – onto our society. Or we may choose to learn and follow principles, guided by experience and nature, that adjust to circumstances without surrendering their ordered reality. We need not share the fate of twentieth-century Europe – cultural breakdown and ideologically driven violence – as we confront the cultural homelessness in our nation.

What would these choices entail, and what would the resulting society look like? To answer these questions, we offer three visions of society, each corresponding to one of the traditions or ideologies we've discussed, and each an option for Americans today. Each vision is stated in terms of a social contract.

It may seem odd or at least unconservative to talk about American society as a contract. After all, contracts reduce social relations to mere words, so aren't they in fact *un*social, lacking in the moral, customary relationships we've written about here? Yet the idea of society as a contract is quite ancient. Medieval and even ancient Roman and Greek writers found it useful to talk about the agreements we make with one another as part of a larger, broader agreement to be and remain one people. The Mayflower Compact, America's earliest foundational document, is a kind of contract. The nature of this contract is particularly interesting because the so-called Pilgrims were in fact Separatists; unlike the Puritans, who sought to purify the church, the Separatists were the most radical Protestants of their age, seeking their own space where they might live freely according to their own demanding Christian principles. In 1620, bound for Virginia but blown off course, the Pilgrims found themselves in a wilderness with no sanctioned governing structures. Unwilling to leave the ordered confines of their ship (where the captain represented political order), they wrote an agreement, signed by all, to bind themselves to live as one people and to support the laws they would pass to order their common lives. This social contract was necessary, they believed, because it is improper to live in a state of nature. There is no more conservative sentiment than this one, expressed by the most radical of all American settlers of the colonial period.

But the contract itself does not create society; it merely builds on preexisting understandings and norms. People live together in peace because of numerous, generally unspoken agreements. In America we agree, or at least once agreed, that we will strive to support ourselves, uphold public peace and morals, take responsibility for our families, and respect the faith of our neighbors and the common faith of our communities. We maintained our common home by agreeing on a common American way of life and our responsibility to maintain that way of life within our natural associations and local communities.

The survival of the American social contract is in peril because we no longer agree on its terms, or even on how to read and alter the terms of any such agreement. Part of the problem is that there is more than one way to read a contract, including a social contract. Three such readings vie for notice and influence in contemporary society. Each can be associated with an influential political philosopher – Edmund Burke, John Locke, and John Rawls. Each is rooted in a different tradition of thought, conceives of society in a different way, and looks to differing social conventions. Two make up the conservative-liberal dynamic that has characterized America from its very beginnings. The third, and most recent, quickly became dominant among our intellectual elites who use it to undermine the other two.

The social contract as conceived by Edmund Burke, the eighteenth-century Anglo-Irish philosopher, statesman, and founder of modern conservatism, is rooted in the natural law, and in the great tradition of Western civilization dating back through the Christian to the Roman era. That of the seventeenth-century English philosopher and essayist John Locke, though earlier than Burke's, is rooted in a more recent, Calvinist tradition of church and local community covenants. In the twentieth century, the American academic philosopher John Rawls presented a social contract as an updated Kantianism but with a spirit found in the radical romanticism of Jean-Jacques Rousseau.

In *Reflections on the Revolution in France*, first published in 1790, Burke wrote about society as a contract between the dead, the living, and those yet to be born. What kind of contract includes the dead? One that is intended to span generations, to bind together a people within a tradition where the links of continuity secure the means of change and improvement. Thus Burke wrote about our inheritance of rights, duties, and social norms as something we take as "an entailed inheritance," meaning something we must receive with thanks from our ancestors and deliver, in at least as good condition, to our descendants. At the core of Burke's contract is a rich conception of partnership. Civilization is a kind of partnership in, among other things, "all science," "all arts" – a "partnership in every virtue, and in all perfection."*

Contracts form partnerships, and most focus on some tangible goal or good for the two parties. But the "social" contract as described by Burke stresses all the key elements of human nature and the means by which they are fulfilled. This contract is physical, legal, and most importantly spiritual; its central purpose is to arrange the diverse parts of the order we inhabit (the visible and the invisible) into something whole, meaningful,

---

* Edmund Burke, *Reflections on the Revolution in France*, edited by J. G. A. Pocock (Indianapolis, IN: Hackett, 1987), 84–85.

and enduring. Burke's contract sustains a multigenerational partnership in the creation and improvement of a given civilization. In addition, this contract provides the structure by which each person's social nature is fulfilled in a diverse but interlocking variety of communities. Weaving together our historical experience and our permanent nature, Burke's conservative contract maintains a home we can share as members of a great, stable, but ever-changing civilizational order.

Locke often is seen as having promoted a radical conception of the social contract, in which isolated individuals come together in a mythical state of nature without any preexisting ties or relations, to make up a government and society out of whole cloth. This is not, however, what Locke suggested. Rather, in his *Second Treatise of Government*, published in 1689, he used the idea of a contract to argue that legitimate government has its roots in the consent of the people.** The people consented not to whatever sort of government might result but to a specific form of government that would continue to seek their consent for legislative actions and that could, in extreme cases, be overthrown by an "appeal to heaven" when it violated the people's basic rights. Locke's thought on this subject was deeply rooted in the experience of early English Calvinist communities (he himself was a dissenting Protestant) that entered covenants (agreements declared before God) to bind themselves together to walk in the ways of their Lord. Moreover, the state of nature he posited was not one of isolated individuals but of families. The first societies, he noted, would have been centered on natural families, with paternal leadership almost insensibly becoming political leadership.

** John Locke, *Second Treatise of Government*, edited by C. B. Macpherson (Indianapolis, IN: Hackett, 1980).

Still, it is important to see Locke's social contract as deeply liberal. That is, he was concerned that the letter of the law be upheld – that those essentially hired to do the people's business be held to the specific terms of the agreement. Where Burke's conservatism looked to the spirit of the law and the customs of the people, Locke's liberalism was more legalistic, rooted in specific language and more formal agreements. Between the two we can see the underlying dynamic of American politics, between the fundamental need for normative relationships and affection and the drive for self-assertion and demand that terms be fulfilled. We haven't the space here to detail the strengths and weaknesses of the liberal tradition. It must suffice for us to note that we hold the conservative tradition to be more deeply rooted in human nature and the demands of a humane social order, but that liberalism remains an integral part of the American story.

Greater innovation is found in the third social contract, that of John Rawls. In his 1971 book, *A Theory of Justice,* Rawls stripped away all the history and social context from the social contract to find the solitary individual unaltered by society and therefore capable of what Rawls deems genuine consent.*** Rawls offers the most abstracting mental exercise possible: what would an individual choose if that individual was completely ignorant of its position in society – of *every* marker of a distinctive self: sex, class, talents, physical limitations, religious and moral beliefs. Such an individual in the "original position" of choosing a social contract from behind this "veil of ignorance" brings no concrete, specific experience to reasoning about what is just. This individual, of course, would have the

---

*** John Rawls, *A Theory of Justice* (Cambridge, MA: Belknap Press of Harvard University Press, 1971).

same reasoning as all other individuals stripped down to their abstract reasoning. Such an individual, Rawls claims, would choose a fair society that provides maximal opportunity for each member subject to an equality of opportunity. The only inequalities a person thinking about justice in this manner would allow would be those that produce disproportionate benefits to the most disadvantaged members of society.

The cold abstraction of Rawls's system produces moral heat against all forms of difference and inequality that don't fit the system. Because this moral ideal does not emerge from a religious system, any specific historical tradition, or anything lived and particular, it is universal and self-evident to its followers. This quality of Rawls's moral vision feeds a deadly combination of abstraction and moral fervor. If we have learned anything over the last two and a half centuries it is that nothing is so dangerous to real, particular, breathing humans as moralism devoted to abstract notions of the good.

Today, American society is in conflict largely because each of these contracts, and the visions of society they foster, is an active, live option for significant groups of people. When reading the Constitution, considering the application of laws, judging customs, and even interacting in the public square, Americans increasingly conceive of our common principles and norms in very different ways, aimed toward very different goals. This does not mean that destructive conflict rooted in mutual alienation is inevitable. Burke and Locke offer us something in common – that humans have nature, and that our nature is fulfilled in institutions that serve our deepest needs. Both of these contracts offer us civilizational homes even as they provide tangible intellectual support for the American tradition of self-rule. Rawls, by contrast, offers us the lure of moral destruction and righteous hatred of all particular things, of all differences, of all beliefs and norms that do not fit with the abstract vision of justice as fairness. Rawls offers a cold and inhumane justice for the present generation and a radical cultural sterility for all future generations, shorn of the past, cut off finally from the story to which they rightfully belong.

That Rawls's vision is radically at odds with the traditions of conservatism and the contextualized individualism of liberalism seems clear. What is less clear is how a society rooted in tradition and historical context is to survive when its elites have imbibed the radical ideology of the Rawlsian contract. Progressives and their leftist progeny have spent the last hundred years attempting to rewrite our social contract. Claiming it always was meant to be a "living" contract, they have reinterpreted the Constitution to suit their vision of the best society at any given moment. In doing so they have proceeded to write over our customary common law with statutes and judicial legislation intentionally undermining our fundamental, natural associations, all in the name of a kind of fairness only Rawls's disembodied selves could truly want.

Each and every one of us is more than a mere self. We are persons with histories. We are by nature social creatures who form and flourish in communities. We are creatures of God, equal in intrinsic dignity but wonderfully different in our desires, capacities, and traditions. We need our families, churches, and local associations – our little platoons in which most of the business of living takes place. America's conservative soul is found in real humans, formed in specific and eccentric ways, who embrace their shared story, who reject golden ages and utopian visions in favor of the hard-won accomplishments of their living tradition. Most of all we love our common home because without it we would be left as mere simulacra of our real selves.

Our government and our ruling classes today are dominated by inhumane, Rawlsian thinking. They have taken from us our home – our confidence in shared expectations and standards of behavior. But they have not destroyed our souls. And the soul of our common lives – the lost but still living soul of American conservatism – can be found if we rebuild the common home in which this soul may reside. Rejecting ideology itself along with the temptation to seek simplistic, ideological solutions to our current situation, we can refocus our energies where they belong, on the particular communities in which we live. Living as we ought, as full participants in the communities of family, church, and local associations, we will by this very mode of life help to rebuild home for ourselves and those we love.

Wider actions are needed as well. We must push back the forces that have multiplied and centralized political power so that communities again can have their natural purpose and space in which to flourish. These communities will fail many times in many things, but only a society in which citizens understand that failure is inevitable in this life, as is the duty to mitigate its effects, can foster the common experience and common feeling that *are* home.

Acknowledgments

This book has its origins in the American Project, a program housed at Pepperdine University's School of Public Policy that aims to reinvigorate American conservatism. As part of that effort, the American Project produced a statement of principles for our time. To provide support for that short signatory document, Pete Peterson, Dean of the School of Public Policy and Director of the American Project, wanted a longer document establishing a historical framework to help explain how the conservative movement had reached this crisis of principles. Such a document would also help to reclaim older, richer, and deeper traditions that have emerged from the American experience.

When it became clear to all involved that this subject is too important and complicated to limit to a single essay, we decided to write this book to marry a historical narrative with a clear and comprehensive statement of principles. Through every phase of this process, Dean Peterson has supported by all possible means the writing of *Coming Home*. This book would not exist without him and the support of the American Project.

Two scholars were particularly helpful to us in thinking through the historical part of the book. Adam MacLeod provided invaluable insights into the common law tradition as it applied to early American history. Adam explained key distinctions and historical context to account for violations of the common law in the case of slavery – distinctions that are almost always overlooked or misunderstood in other accounts. Darren Staloff's sharp criticisms, rejection of all academic cant – particularly if it is deferential to dubious intellectual fashions – and his dedication to empirical evidence helped us escape any lingering need to signal our virtue to the doyens of our academic discipline. Darren and Adam both reinforced our desire to write truthfully, with the candor and simplicity appropriate for our intellectually disordered times. Bruce Frohnen owes special thanks to Allan and Harriette Fox for guidance and support.

As we neared completion of the manuscript, several people read portions or all of our work and offered encouragement and advice. We want particularly to thank Wilfred McClay, Victor Davis Hanson, Fred Siegel, and Rob Waters, each of whom encouraged us to place this book with a trade publisher and who unanimously recommended Encounter Books as the ideal house for our work. We are very glad of their guidance.

We want to thank the Encounter team, who provided us with the best support in all of our experiences in book publishing. Katherine Wong has guided us through the process with wisdom and enthusiasm. Our copyeditor, Jessica Hornik Evans, saved us from several infelicities and numerous errors. We owe a special thanks to Roger Kimball for seeing the potential in our book.

Finally, a book on home and American conservatism ought to be deeply connected to the first and most defining community: family. So it is with us. And so we have dedicated this book to our wives and children, who give our lives deeper meanings, higher purposes, and the joys that express our distinctive place in God's story. They truly make us home.

Index

A NOTE ON THE TYPE

COMING HOME *has been set in Pegasus, a roman type designed in 1937 by Berthold Wolpe, the German-born calligrapher, type designer, book designer, and educator. Wolpe is best known for his extensive career at Faber and Faber in London, where he developed a distinctive (and widely imitated) treatment of lettering and typography for the firm's dust jackets and covers, much of it anchored by his handsome Albertus types. Pegasus – revived and expanded by Matthew Carter in 1980 and redrawn in 2017 by Toshi Omagari for Monotype – encapsulates much of the spirit of Wolpe's calligraphic practice. Particularly noteworthy are subtle inconsistencies in stroke weight and serif shape, features that give the characters a pleasing, organic warmth and rich color on the page.*

DESIGN & COMPOSITION BY CARL W. SCARBROUGH